End paper: *Duke August of Braun-schweig-Lüneburg (1579 – 1666) playing chess. Copperplate engraving by Jacob van der Heyden (1573 – 1645) taken from: Gustavus Selenus' "Chess or the Game of Kings," Leipzig, 1616.*

Above: *Knight, Russian, turned from bone, 18th century (Historical Museum, Moscow).*

Pages 2/3:

Queen: *China, ivory, 19th century.*

Fou *(jester on horseback): France, ivory, early 16th century.*

Bishop: *Scandinavian, bone (walrus), around 1200.*

King: *Scandinavian, walrus tusk, around 1200.*

ROSWIN FINKENZELLER

WILHELM ZIEHR

EMIL M. BÜHRER

ESS

A celebration of 2000 years

KEY PORTER BOOKS

General direction:
Motovun (Switzerland) Co-Publishing Company Ltd., Lucerne

Pictorial support:
Collection Dr. Ernst and Sonya Böhlen, Switzerland
Collection David Hafler, Merion, Pa.

Airbrush illustrations:
Jovan Stojanović, Snežana Něić and Bessa Publishing Company, Belgrade

Translation from German by Anglia Translations, Catherine Badger, Liz Crossley

Canadian Cataloguing in Publication Data

Finkenzeller, Roswin, 1934-
    Chess: a celebration of 2000 years

Translation of: Schach: 2000 Jahre Spiel-Geschichte.
ISBN 1-55013-169-9

I.   Chess – History. I. Ziehr,
      Wilhelm, 1938-
II.   Bührer, Emil M. (Emil Martin),
      1913-
III. Title.

GV1317.F5613 1989
794.1'09   C89-094466-0

Lithography:
Lanarepro, Lana/Meran
Printing and Binding:
Rotolito Lombarda, Pioltello/Milano
Typesetting:
F. X. Stückle, Ettenheim

Printed in Italy

CONTENTS

Opposite: *Highly magnified detail of a chess piece. The king stands in front of warriors wearing coats of mail and carrying shields and swords. The warriors are grouped around their king and ruler (German, 14th century, ivory). Through the ages and in every culture, the "Game of Kings" has appealed to the imagination of craftsmen in every society. They have created chess pieces from priceless materials in an amazing variety of interpretations.*

FOREWORD

Napoleon standing with his arms folded, from a chess game with cast iron chessmen. One set portrayed the French and the other the Prussians (Berlin, circa 1825).

Chess fascinates artists and eccentrics, almost magically attracts members of all classes of society, delights millionaires and have-nots. Yet chess is also able to bring forth artists and eccentrics itself, to make millionaires of inspired players and to give victories not worth a penny to have-nots. This has been true for some two thousand years. Over time many influences have gradually shaped and changed a game of such great complexity; thus, chess historians do not search for an inventor, but rather for a culture sophisticated enough to have developed such a game and integrated it into daily life.

Whoever starts to play chess and goes beyond the basics can only desist with difficulty. Someday, he will also wonder about the origins of the game, about the old masters, the great chess nations and the politics of the chessboard. Yet the student of chess history finds himself in a peculiar situation: the further back in time he goes, the more the game loses precision in the modern sense, yet the more interesting its cultural history becomes; the behavior of chess players, regardless of their race, nationality, or place in time, has remained unchanged for the most part. Psychological strengths and weaknesses, brilliant ideas,

strange miscalculations, blindness and farsightedness, discipline and improvisation, stubborn insistence in the face of unambiguous rules: these have always been evident. At some point we realize that the game's attraction does not lie in social contact between players, but, generally speaking, is to be found in opposition. Everywhere, we encounter opposites: black and white, victory and defeat, right and wrong, attack and defense, logic and its refutation by genius. We ourselves embody only a part of the opposites possible, which is what lures us back to the board. The existential component of the player's intellectual achievement raises chess above all other games. In this respect it is a lesser issue, or could be considered of secondary importance, whether the Indians or the Chinese invented chess. Its invention ennobles the human race, and the game of chess became and remains a possession of all mankind.

In the past and the present, chess is a living game, a game subject to fashion and change. Even the 1988 rules of the World Chess Federation (FIDE) demonstrate this indirectly. In Article 1, indeed, in all of the following articles, the wording is precise; for example, "Chess is played by two opponents who move pieces ('chessmen') on a square surface called a 'chessboard'." On the other hand, the indescribable variety of this game is mentioned explicitly in the introduction to the book of rules: "The rules of chess cannot regulate all situa-

plicated they can make a position and what psychological tricks they incorporate in their moves. As early as 1936, Capablanca was already astonished at how chess had changed in our century, recalling his 1911 tournament: "At that time, we hardly knew anything about the qualities of our adversaries, but we were capable of accomplishing an enormous amount of work. Today, we know our opponents through and through, but, ah, our capabilities are no longer the same. Then, we were nervous and often lost our composure. Today we are cool and controlled, and only an earthquake could disconcert us. We have more experience, yet less strength."

The history of chess is still written and scientific research into the game actively conducted. Unknown records about the game's origins may be discovered in the ruins of advanced early civilizations; excavations may uncover new connections. There is much, however, that we will never know with absolute certainty. People can carry their knowledge thousands of kilometers, without anyone ever being able to prove which paths they took.

This book provides a most advanced summary of the status of research into the royal game's beginnings and paths of dissemination. It traces the game's significant developmental stages. The authors were guided by the love of the game as well as its cultural history in writing this book.

tions that may arise in the course of a game, and also not answer all administrative questions. Chess lives in its differences. Between the intellectual capacities of international masters and grandmasters and the simple enjoyment of amateurs, there lie milestones, libraries of literature on openings, hundreds of recorded master games. Karpov's or Kasparov's opening with the king's pawn is only formally the same move when made by an average player. Worlds of knowledge and ignorance are being broached. Chess masters often demonstrate to astonished chess fans how com-

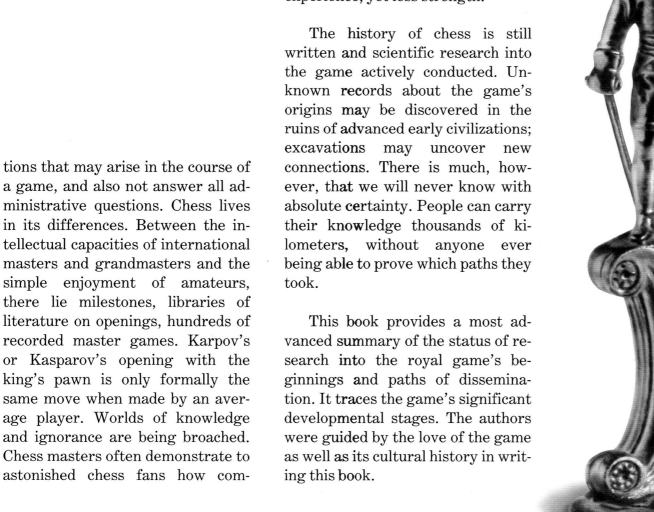

"Chess ist not *like* life …
Chess *is* life.
Just like the theatre."

*Fernando Arrabal
during the "Battle of the Giants,"
Bobby Fischer against Boris Spassky
in Reykjavik 1972.*

FACT AND FICTION

*Miniature and text from a manuscript written by Jacobo da Cessole (1407). Bavarian State Library, Munich.
"Two wise men (bishops) are to have the following form on the chessboard; they are both to be seated on chairs holding books in their laps, as they represent the judge and the lawmaker/instructor."*

Opposite: *The world of chess is also represented in the modern art world. The painting by Sami Briss, "The Chess King," painted in 1976, shows the King leaning on a chess-board, holding a pawn in his hand.*

The game of chess has spread throughout the world to become an accepted part of our culture. Mankind has created no other game that comes anywhere near its level of excellence. However, when we refer to chess, we should consider the many different levels at which it is played. There is the game of the casual player, an intriguing intellectual recreation, one quickly discovers, but there is also the game of the serious player who strives to win in competition. At whatever level it is played, everyone agrees that it is a fascinating game. The brilliance attained by the great chess masters may never be reached by the average player, but he appreciates the master's game just as a piano student appreciates a concert pianist's rendition of Chopin's nocturnes.

Any player who personally wants to experience and appreciate the beauty, vitality, and order of chess as it is played today must either be a born player, or at least be willing to learn more than just the correct moves of the chess pieces. Worldwide publicity given to the chess masters, grandmasters and to the incredible historical evolution of chess over many centuries has resulted in a fascination in the game not only for those who play but also for all those interested in physical and mental excellence. The famous American statesman and author Benjamin Franklin wrote in 1779 in the first American book on chess, *Morals of Chess,* that the game is not only a pleasant pastime but also an illustration of life, its struggles

and competitiveness, its good and evil. He believed that chess teaches "Foresight, by having to plan ahead ... vigilance, by having to keep watch over the whole chessboard ... caution, by having to restrain ourselves from making hasty moves ... and finally, we learn from chess the greatest maxim in life, that even when everything seems to be going badly for us we should not lose heart but, always hoping for a change for the better, steadfastly continue searching for the solutions to our problems."

The Russian Chess Master J. Rochlin was no less sincere when he stated in 1954 that: "We do not claim that chess of itself has tangible, practical merits, but, as is the case in every art form, we can see that the creativity required when playing the game has produced definite cultural values which, in their totality, have made a valuable contribution to the treasure chest of global culture ... When we study the history of chess and the centuries of chess literature, we have to acknowledge that the quality and level of mankind's achievements as well as the influence of the world around us and the influences of art, are all mirrored in the creative exercise of the game of chess."

Chess history can be divided into three clearly marked periods which correspond to the three stages in the development of the game. The first period covers those centuries when the game began to differ from the many other similar board games from India and the Orient. During this period a complex set of rules

emerged, leading to a game requiring a higher degree of tactical skill. The second period began when the game spread into Europe after its conquest of the Arab world. Chess made extensive inroads in the Middle Ages but it was only from the 16th century that a considerable volume of written reference to the game appeared, a development which marked the beginning of modern chess. This literature immortalized the first recorded names in chess history: Damiano, Ruy López and Gioacchino Greco. The games of the chess masters began systematically to improve. Chess strategy became a subject to be studied and numerous books were written giving instructions on how to play the opening moves of the game. As an intellectual activity, chess was compared to art and science. The games played in Paris at the "Café de la Régence" and in London clubs mark the high point of the period: its rising star was François Philidor.

The last phase in the game's development is bound together with the era of the great chess masters. It began with the International Tournament held in London in 1851 and has continued to the present day.

Chess enthusiasts first became interested in the origin of chess after it had developed a certain degree of perfection with a set of clearly-defined rules; and after it had become not only a socially acceptable game but also a well-regulated game played by masters in local and international competitions.

A contemporary portrait of François André Danican Philidor (1726–1795). Philidor was the most famous chess-player of his time. His brilliant games in Paris and London attracted major attention. Both cities became centers of European chess.

EARLY LEGENDS

A fresco from the tomb of Queen Nefertari of Egypt in Karnak (circa 1250 B.C.. The queen is seen at a board game in which figures similar to towers were used.

There are many beautiful legends about the origin of chess and each one pays tribute to the various people it mentions. The legends confirm that the development of the game was considered to be a notable achievement and one that was highly valued by the civilizations of Asia and of classical antiquity. Frescoes depicting pharaohs and members of the ruling class seated at game boards with game pieces similar to those used in chess have been discovered in several Egyptian tombs. One example can be seen in the tomb of Queen Nefertari dated around 1250 B.C., and another, a caricature of Ramses III from the 13th century B.C., depicts him playing a game that resembles chess. In the Egyptian Museum in Berlin, there is a figure resembling the rook which has been attributed to the 3rd century. These objects have led to the overly hasty conclusion that the game of chess originated in Egypt.

Closer examination, however, has shown that although board games similar to chess were in use, there is no evidence that these games fit into the historical evolution of chess. The Egyptians, played board game with 30 squares and 12 pieces, and another one with 144 squares and 48 pieces. The boards were usually rectangular and the squares all of one color. For a long time another favorite theory of chess historians was that the Greeks, in particular Palamedes, had invented the game. Palamedes, so the story goes, invented the game in an attempt to assuage the boredom of camp life during the long years of the unsuccessful siege of Troy. He was the son of the King of Euboea and the grandson of Poseidon and was credited with many discoveries.

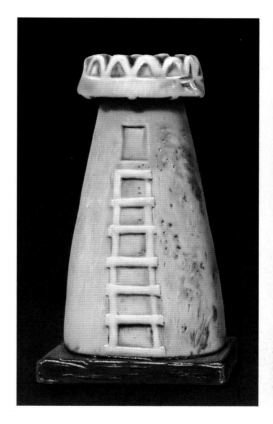

Figures in ivory in the shape of towers were known in Egypt from ancient times (3000 B.C.), but they were definitely not used for chess.

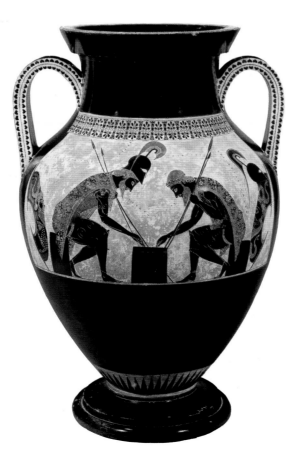

The famous Exekias Amphora from the Villa Giulia in Rome, 5th century B.C. For a long time, chess historians believed that the Greeks had invented the "Game of Kings," but more recent research provides evidence that the game originated in the Far East.

11

Among these were the alphabet, figures and the decimal system, and a system of weights and measures. The legends also give him credit for having invented both chess and dice games to keep his idle troops occupied. The basis for this legend is a painted vase which portrays the famous warriors, Achilles and Ajax, playing a game. The vase, an amphora made by Exekias in the 5th century B.C., is displayed in the Villa Giulia in Rome. The painting

chess was presented to the Gods of Olympus at the wedding of Oceanus (the Latin name for the sea-god Poseidon) to the Earth Mother. In 1763, this classical fable inspired Sir William Jones (1746–1794), a British orientalist, to propose the nymph Caïssa as the Muse of Chess (*Caissa, or the Game of Chess,* 1772).

The Italians of the Renaissance period were the chief adherents to the theory that chess had its origin in Greece; whereas the Spanish, who were the strongest opponents of the Italian chess masters in the 16th century, held that the Persians, the Greeks' enemy, were the inventors. In the 5th century the Persians were campaigning against the Greeks and there is no doubt that they were a highly civilized nation, but chess historians have rejected the theory that they invented chess. Both Babylonia and, more believably, China have also been suggested as the land of origin but, according to our present knowledge, China only took over and adapted the game. "Elephant Chess" (*Xiang Qi*), as the game was known in China, was played on an almost square board, eight squares by nine squares, that had a neutral zone called the river border. The playing pieces were round, flat, inscribed stones. These stones were placed on the corners of the squares, not on the squares. The figures on the stones were quite unusual, *e.g.,* cannons, soldiers and horses. Chinese chess spread through Korea and on to Japan where it was called "Shogi — The Game of the Generals." The board was nine squares by nine

The pieces of the Chinese "Elephant Game" Xiang Qi:

1. The King *(red denotes "strategist," green "commander")*

2. The Minister *(the inscription means "adviser")*

3. The General *(green denotes "elephant," red "chancellor")*

4. The Horse

5. The Wagon

6. The Cannon

7. The 5 Soldiers

on the vase, however, only proves that the two heroes were seated in front of a board game; they were certainly not playing chess. Nevertheless, the first French chess magazine, published in 1836, bore the name *La Palamède* in honor of this supposed inventor.

In 1513, Marcus Hieronymus Vida, the Bishop of Alba (1485 to 1566), wrote a Latin poem "Scacchia ludus" in which it was implied that the newly invented game of

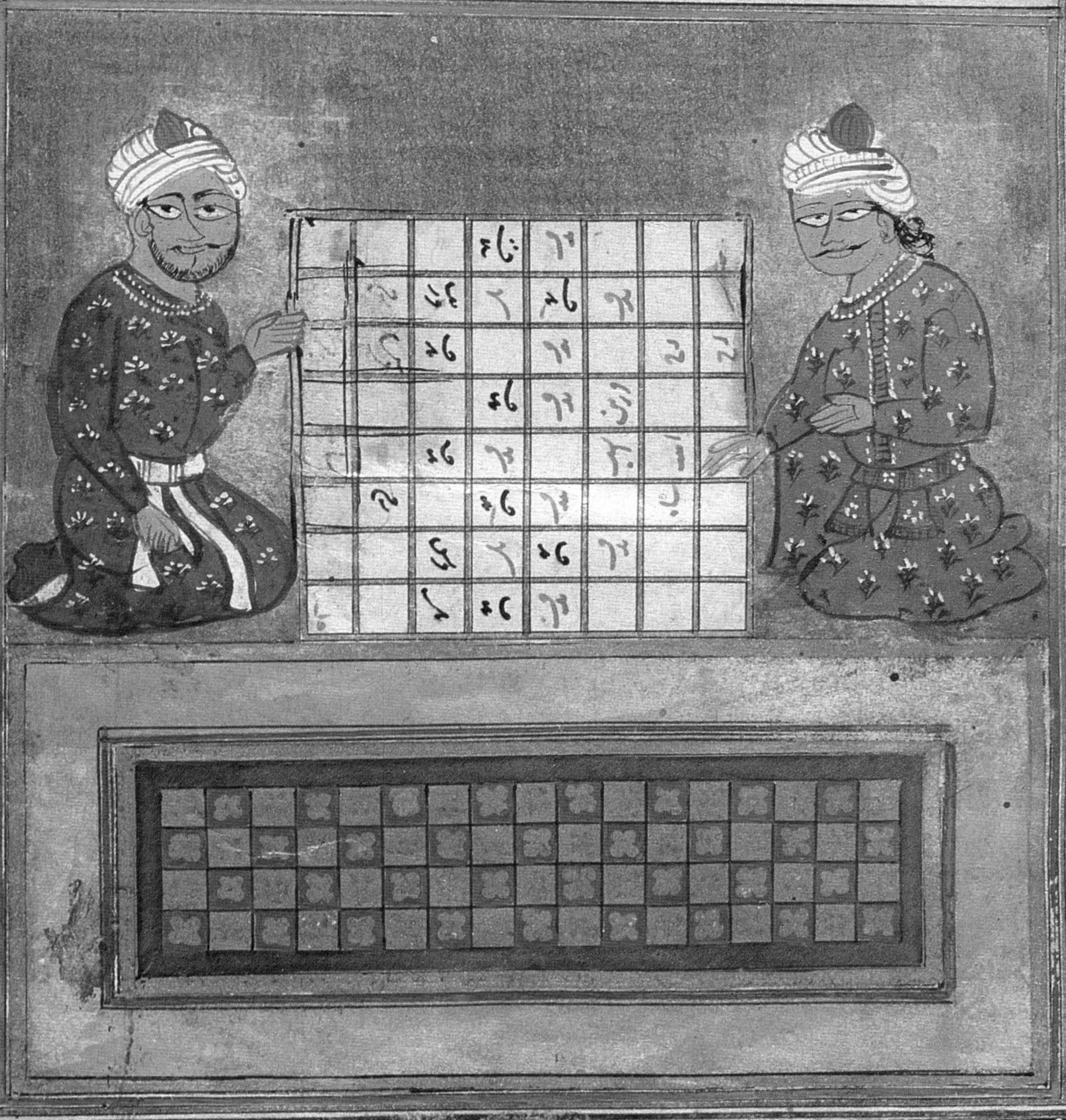

The positions of the playing pieces in Indian four-player chess. The Indians were familiar with chess for 2 as well as for 4 players.

squares. Each player had twenty playing pieces of eight different kinds which were placed on three rows.

Chess, as it was played in Persia and Arabia, had reached a very high standard long before the game reached Europe. Old Persian and Arabian documents of the 9th century claimed that India was the country where chess originated. Modern analytical research is in agreement: the oldest written evidence comes from India, linguistic studies indicate the area around the Ganges, and archaeological finds of old chess figures also point to Far Eastern cultures. In the 7th century A.D., the Indian poet Bana wrote a poem in Sanskrit which he dedicated to King Sriharsha (606–647). The verses praise the King as a "Prince of Peace" because the only wars in the country were between the bees as they searched for pollen, and the only armies *(Tschaturanga)* were those that marched on the 64 squares of the chessboard. The fact that a poet ventured to use such a comparison certainly means that it would have been universally understood and leads us to assume that chess already had a long tradition and was known and understood by the general public. It certainly takes more than a few centuries for a game like chess to evolve, especially when we consider that without modern methods of communication it would have spread very slowly. After careful consideration there is every reason to believe that we can look for the origin of chess in the centuries before the birth of Christ.

THE INDIAN GAME

There is historical proof that early Indian chess was not the same chess that had found its way into Persia in the 6th century. Indian chess was a board game that probably resembled many others of that period, but it had unique features that captured the imagination of the players more than any other game of its time. This "forefather of chess" was played on 64 squares by four players, but they played with red, green, yellow and black dice. The assignment of playing pieces seems strange to us today. Each player had eight pieces: a king, an elephant (equivalent to our bishop), a knight, a rook (in the shape of a boat or a chariot), and four soldiers (pawns). The king, elephant, knight, rook and soldier were advanced according to the number thrown on the four sided oblong dice. The players tried to win the game by capturing another king's throne. The game was played in pairs, the winner being the player who was able to capture two kings or even bring home all four kings. Elephants and boats as chess figures were still used in Russia in the 16th century, and they can be traced back to the old Indian playing pieces. Chess was a war game. The old Sanskrit word for chess, *Tschaturanga (Tschatur* meaning four

A miniature from the chess book of Alfonso the Wise, 1283. The illustration refers to the legend of the origin of chess; three Indian seers bring a chess game and a dice game to the Persian king who is portrayed here as a Christian ruler.

and *anga* meaning part or section), clearly indicates that the name was derived from the four army divisions in existence when Alexander the Great defeated the Indian King Poros at the battle on the Hydaspes. Greek historians gave detailed accounts of the Indian army divisions; in addition to the infantry there were the cavalry, war chariots and elephants. These four army divisions correspond to the figures used in the game from which chess developed, *i.e.*, in four-dice chess. The fact that chess figures corresponded to the army classification supports the argument that the game originated either in the 4th century B.C. at the time of Alexander the Great or at the time of the Gupta dynasty in the 4th and 5th centuries A.D., because in both periods army divisions were identical to the chess pieces. The characteristic move of the knight must already have been known. However, it is not known

15

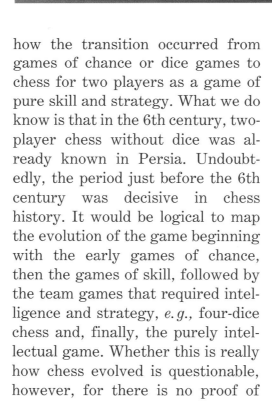

Indian chess pieces were carved from priceless materials e.g. ebony and fine woods. In the 18th and 19th centuries chess sets portrayed Indians in their traditional robes and wagons or even the troops of the British East India Company.

Above right: *The so-called "Juggernaut" wagon, an additional figure in Indian chess.*

Far right: *The rook was also portrayed as a ship, Russian ivory carving from 1770.*

how the transition occurred from games of chance or dice games to chess for two players as a game of pure skill and strategy. What we do know is that in the 6th century, two-player chess without dice was already known in Persia. Undoubtedly, the period just before the 6th century was decisive in chess history. It would be logical to map the evolution of the game beginning with the early games of chance, then the games of skill, followed by the team games that required intelligence and strategy, *e.g.,* four-dice chess and, finally, the purely intellectual game. Whether this is really how chess evolved is questionable, however, for there is no proof of

when this all happened nor of how long each period lasted. We search for logical explanations precisely because we do not have any proof.

Indian chess had its own rules until very recent times. Even in 1928 when the undisputed Indian chess master, Mir Malik Sultan Khan played in England, he was not familiar with the double move of the pawn, the *en passant* capture, and castling. It did not take him long to master these moves and he went on to win the English Championship in 1929, and was able to repeat his victory again in 1931 and 1933. He defeated José Raúl Capablanca and the grandmaster Savielly Tartakower. After losing to the Czech-Soviet grand master Salo Flohr, he returned to India at the end of the 30's and disappeared from the international chess scene. Tartakover praised the originality and depth of his knowledge, but what Khan lacked in his game was the rich diversity of modern chess. This was a disadvantage in his confrontations with the top world players, a disadvantage that he was not able to

overcome. Chess as it is played today is more closely related to the old Persian game and its modifications than to the Indian game. The Persians retained the old Indian names; *Tschaturanga* became the similar-sounding *Schatrandsch,* Sanskrit and Persian being closely related languages. Chess to the Persians was a battle of kings and their troops. When a player attacked his opponent's king he respectfully called *Shah* (the Persian word for king), which meant "king beware." If the king was defeated and in a hopeless position, rather than defeated in the sense of being killed, the attacker called *Shahmat* (*mat* meaning helpless). Although the

Persians probably added the queen to the game, fate did not leave them much time to make any further changes. In 641, the last Persian king of the Sasanian dynasty was forced to flee from the conquering Arab army and thereby lost his kingdom. Although the Sasanian kings had ruled over parts of Indian territory at various times in their past and there had been close contact between the two peoples, Indian four-player chess is not mentioned in Persian sources, nor is any reference ever made to the use of dice in Persian chess. Chess in its most developed form, that of two-player Indian chess, was the game that was adopted by the Persians. The Indian names and expressions were translated into Persian and game pieces like the elephant and chariot were adapted to Persian culture: the elephant became the horse, and the chariot became a bird's head because the Indian word for chariot sounded to the Persians like their word for the fabled giant bird, the *Ruhk*. These new Persian terms strongly influenced Arabian chess and even early European chess. For example, the Indian word for king, *raja,* became the Persian *shah* and this term was directly adopted by the Arab world. Similarly, the call *Shahmat* was taken over by the Arabs. Also, the modern German *Rochade,* for castling, can be traced back to the word *Rukh,* and in the 17th century, reference was still made to *Roche* in German chess literature. In this way, the game and the designations given to its figures began to conform in terminology.

"There is a widespread notion that the faculty of devising combinations in chess cannot be acquired, but depends rather on an inborn power of calculation and imagination. Every experienced player knows, however, that this general opinion is erroneous, and that most combinations, indeed, practically all of them, are devised by recalling known elements, such as the famous Bishop sacrifices on white's f7, or h7, which will not give the advanced player anything much to think about. That the power of combination can be developed by study really seems very natural after one considers both its components separately. No one will doubt that the ability to think a thing out tediously in advance can be practised, and as for the imagination which furnishes the necessary ideas and surprises for the combination, it has been proved by psychologists that it cannot offer anything absolutely new, but, contenting itself with combining familiar elements, can be developed by increasing knowledge of such elements."

Richard Réti in
"Masters of the Chess-board"

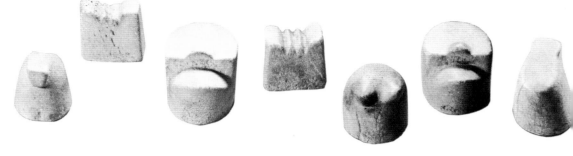

Right: *8th/9th century chess pieces of carved bone. In this period chess figures were often modeled on the more simple forms of the Arabian pieces. From l. to r.: knight, war wagon (rook), king, war wagon (rook), knight, vizir (queen) and soldier (pawn).*

The silk road, which accounted for the spread of chess, passed through Persia and the great Persian poet, Firdusi, in his epic *Shahname* (King's Book), related the legend of how chess was brought to Persia and its royal court. One day, an Indian legation

the rules of the game were only known in India. However, if the Persians were able to discover the correct positions and moves of the game, and at the same time unravel its rules, he would discharge them from their duty of paying him tribute and taxes, as wisdom was

Two Moorish Arabian ladies playing chess. While they are playing, a third woman entertains them on a seven-stringed guitar. A miniature from the Alfonso the Wise manuscript.

arrived at the court of King Khosrau of Persia (532–578), who was also known as Khosrau the Just. Among the many gifts sent by the Indian king was the as yet unknown game of chess. In a message accompanying the board and figures, the Indian ruler stated that

more valuable than worldly goods. The Indian envoy then told them the names of the game pieces and added that the game could be likened to a battle. If the Persians were unable to solve the puzzle of the game, they would not be considered equal to the Indians and would therefore have to

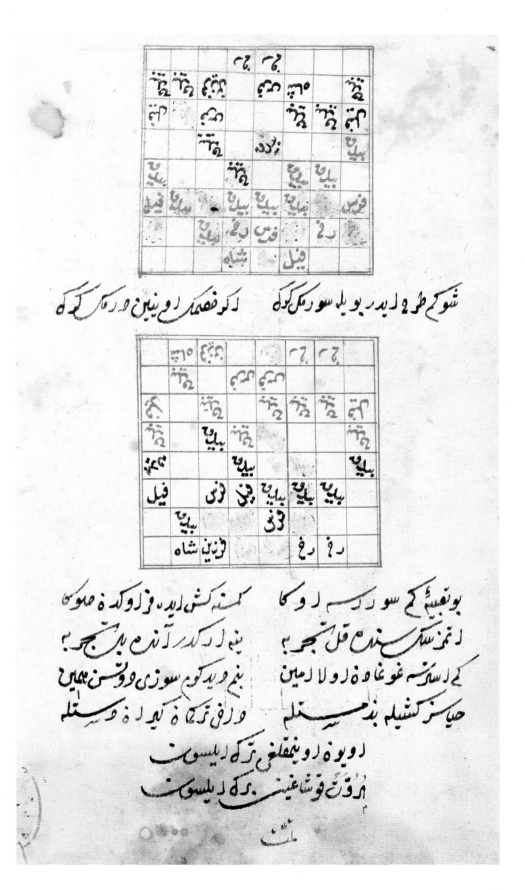

pay tribute. The Persian wise men were given eight days in which to unlock the game's secrets. The wise men were unsuccessful, but a vizier (chief minister) working on his own managed to discover the solution to the puzzle. The king called the court before him, and in the presence of the Indian legation, explained how to set up the figures. In this way, the Persians proved themselves equal to the Indian game, which then spread throughout the kingdom.

THE ARABIAN GAME AND PRINCESS DILARAM

No sooner had the Arabs conquered Persia, Central Asia and North Africa than they themselves started playing the Persian game, which they named *Shatranj*. Their literature already mentions the game in records dating back to the 8th century. Chess was referred to in many legends, poems and daily expressions. It was a pupular game at the courts of the caliphs. Numerous books were written about chess, the first that can be classed as being scientific treatises. Similarities between chess and mathematics were scrutinized. From this period, we have the first written references to competitions, tournaments and the names of the first professional players. The earliest known masters in chess history were all Arabs: Al-

> "The tactician must know
> what to do whenever something needs doing;
> the strategist must know
> what to do when nothing needs doing."
>
> *Savielly Tartakover*

Below: *Arabian players often set up their boards by choosing the positions for their chess pieces (known as Tabija). This practice had a definite influence on the character of the game. Certain starting positions led either to decidedly aggressive games or to contests of position.*

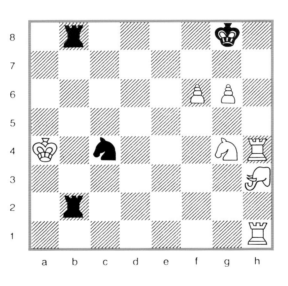

Above right: *The Checkmate of the Arabian Princess Dilaram depicts the beautiful legend of the sacrifice of the rooks. The elephant, in many ways similar to a bishop, is able to move ahead two squares and bid check. White advanced his rook to h8 which is then taken by the king. The elephant moves from h3 to f6 (Retreat Chess), the King to g8, the second rook is sacrificed on h8, the king attacks again at which the pawn advances from g6 to g7 and bids check, the king moves to g8, and then the knight successfully bids mate from h6.*

Adli, Ar-Razi and As-Suli, who died in 946. Al-Adli, who died circa 850, published a treatise in which he made public his method and described the many different strategies in use at the time, as well as disclosing his solutions to problem positions admired by many people in the past. In 847, he lost in a contest against Ar-Razi that took place at the court of Caliph Al-Mutawakkil. Ar-Razi, who lived until 850, was revered as the greatest player of his time. He wrote a book with the descriptive title *Playing Chess with Elegance.* Arabian writings not only praised the beauty of chess, the authors of the period also recommended chess as an educational aid in the development of logical thinking. They also held the opinion that chess could lead to an insight into things to come, could enhance friendships, and also protect against loneliness. The Arabs became enthusiastic players and all classes of society were enchanted by the game. Even the caliphs played and were very generous

to the masters, showering them with gold and gifts. As-Suli's fame was so great that he was later credited with having invented the game. Almost 300 years later it was still considered a great honor for a master to be likened to As-Suli.

Of course, defeating a caliph at the chessboard was not without its dangers; it could be equally difficult to play in such a way as to let the caliph win on purpose. Royal wrath could destroy the hapless player. However, the caliphs were usually spectators, and they enjoyed watching their favorites at the game, but the favorite who lost his game could quickly find himself out of favor. After Al-Maswardi lost a game to As-Suli the caliph informed him, "Your rosewater has been changed to urine." But not only caliphs and their sons played chess in Arabian lands, princesses also played. In fact, it was customary for ladies to play chess. Many poems recount how chess players had been so distracted by the beauty of a female opponent that they lost the game. All too often chess became a game of love filled with many exciting variations. The famous Caliph Harun al Raschid was defeated by both his sister and his clever vizier. The spirit that prevailed in the Arabian chess world is illustrated by the wonderful legend of Princess Dilaram. She was the favorite wife of the Grand Vizier Murwadi, who, although an ardent chess player, was also a very average one. He had lost a fortune in an unlucky game, then gambled away his remaining possessions and finally even set Dilaram as

"It's not a question
of finding the best moves,
but of playing to a rational plan."

Eugène Snosko-Borovsky

the prize. Filled with anxiety, Dilaram watched as her husband's game progressively worsened until it was generally agreed that his position was hopeless. Suddenly the clever princess saw a series of moves that would win the game and save her life. Her desperate husband, on the point of conceding defeat, heard her whispered words, "Sacrifice your rooks and you will save your wife." Murwadi followed her advice: he moved the first rook to h8 to check, then, after the black king had captured this rook, Murwadi was able to move his elephant from h3 to f5 thus enabling the second rook, which had been waiting in the background on h1, to also check. Blocked by the white pawns on the 7th row, the black king was forced to return to g8. Murwadi then had no alternative but to sacrifice his second rook on h8. The elephant then controlled h7 so he was able to advance his pawn to g6 and check the black king, who hastily moved back to g8. Those watching the game thought that White's position was even worse than before – he had lost two rooks, whereas Black still held his original position. Nevertheless, before his opponent had a chance to check, the Grand Vizier was able to checkmate the black king. Murwadi moved his knight to h6 to mate, a move that could not be parried.

Chess, as played in Arabia, already demanded a keen understanding of position and a well-planned strategy aiming at checkmate. By this time, the essential form of chess was, in most respects, the same

game that would eventually make its way into Europe. The differences were mainly in the moves allowed, the names of the pieces, and their positioning at the beginning of the game according to the nature of the game to be played. The arrangement of setting up the pieces before the game began was known as *Tabija* an expression still used in the opening play of Russian masters. Arabian players were also familiar with the blindfold game, and players

Miniature from the chess book of Alfonso the Wise, 1283, an advanced work of early European chess literature, which owes its quality to high Arabian standards. Advised by two wise men, King Alfonso dictated his book to a secretary.

were already rated according to the level of their playing ability. *Mansuben* were extremely popular — problem endgame positions with several moves to checkmate. A wealth of literature on this subject has been preserved.

وتحمل القفص والحمالة والفرس والبالة انها لفظت على اللزم فأضاعت بعض مذ زجها
ونشد مذ زجها لما داننى قرنت بالرقعة درهما وقطعة وقلت لها ان رغبت فى المشوق المعلم
واشرت الى الحب الدرهم فوجى بالسر المههم وان ابيت ان نترجى فخذى القطعة وابيرجن

فالن الى استخلاض البدر النم والابلح الهم وقالت دع جدالك ونل عما بدالك فاسطع
طلع الشيخ بلدنه والسعر والسعر وابيح بردنه فقالت ان الشيخ من اهل شروج وهو الذى وفى

SPREADING INTO EUROPE

At the beginning of the 8th century, the Arab world extended as far as the Iberian Peninsula, Sicily and Sardinia. Europe was greatly enriched by this contact with Arabian culture and civilization. The Arab world was far ahead of the Occident in adopting the material goods, science and technical achievements of the Mediterranean countries, Rome and the Byzantine. It was only in the 13th

and Sicily, which is how chess made its way into Europe. This can be confirmed by the oldest written references dated 1008 and 1058. Between 1008 and 1010, Count Ermengaud of Urgel wrote his last will and testament stipulating that on his death his priceless rock crystal chess pieces should be given to the Cloister Saint-Gilles-du Gard near Tîmes. The Count's sister-in-law from Barcelona, Ermesind, also willed a chess set to the same cloister. The first Western European book dedicated to chess and its strategy was published in Spain in 1283. Titled *The Book of Chess, Dice and Board Games*, it is also

Opposite: Because it was forbidden in the Koran to portray people and animals, Arabian art was rich in ornamental forms, calligraphy and abstract patterns. Europe has the Arabian world to thank for passing on its rich cultural heritage of classical antiquity and its exemplary wealth of music and poetry. European civilization in the Middle Ages was greatly enriched by the cultural exchange with the Arabian Emirates in Spain and the passing on of knowledge via Sicily (Emperor Frederick II of Hohenstaufen). Chess was only one of many areas in which the Arabian influence made itself felt.

and 14th centuries that cultural stagnation set in upon the Islamic world. The relationship between the Occident and the Orient was not only characterized by battles and atrocities between Moslems and Christians; there were also cultural exchanges between them in Spain

known as the Alfonso Manuscript. King Alfonso X, the Wise, probably only wrote the foreword, but the document has been associated with his name ever since. This manuscript is important to chess history because it linked later vital innovations with the Arabian method of

Miniatures from the famous Alfonso the Wise manuscript: the Christian knights with their lances, flags and pennants. After the Islamic conquest of the Iberian Peninsula in 711 the relationship between Arabs and Spaniards was not always one of warfare. There were also periods of rapprochement and peaceful coexistence.

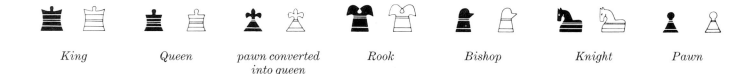

| King | Queen | pawn converted into queen | Rook | Bishop | Knight | Pawn |

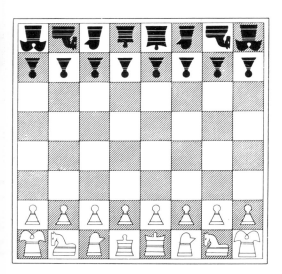

A diagram of pieces positioned on the board — from the Chess book of Alfonso the Wise who lived from 1221 to 1284. The Book of Chess, Dice- and Board Games *was completed in 1283. King Alfonso probably only wrote the foreword. The kings were placed in the positions used today, i.e. e1 and e8.*

Opposite: *An illustration of one of the numerous chess problems based on the Arabian Mansuben (problem endgame positions) from the "Codex Alfonso" which presents numerous, similar problem exercises with explanations and solutions to the problems (preserved in the Escorial).*

play, *e.g.*, the ways in which the chess pieces could be moved, in particular the development of the queen's characteristic advance. By the 11th century, chess was generally known throughout Europe. There were several probable routes into Europe: chess could have spread to the north from Sicily and Southern Italy, where Arabian influence was still very strong; or it could have pushed its way into Central Europe via Asia Minor, the Balkans or the Byzantine (East Roman) Empire. It is also possible that it reached Central Europe via the trade routes from Central Asia through the southern steppes of early Russia. Chess figures found in Samarkand and Fergana of the 7th and 8th centuries can definitely be traced back to Persia to a very early period of the Persian game. From here they spread further. By 1000 A.D., chess had probably made its way into the region of ancient Kiev Rus, the oldest of the Russian states, which lay on the regularly used Viking trade routes. Not only did the Vikings carry Arabian coins and statues of Buddha back to their Scandinavian homeland, there is evidence that they also carried chess pieces. Similar wide-ranging trade routes ensured that, by the 11th and 12th centuries, chess had made its way as far as Iceland. An Icelandic saga of 1155 tells the story of the Danish king, Knut the Great, playing chess in 1027.

Arabian chess pieces were found in many areas of Central Europe during the 11th and 12th centuries. They could well have originated in Southern Europe but it is just as likely that they were brought from the Far East by the Vikings. Chess, as played in Europe from the late Middle Ages, did not have a universally accepted set of rules nor would it have been played with a uniform degree of skill. Players in this period were mainly interested in the endgame. They were still strongly influenced by the long Arab tradition of solving endgame problems, the so called *Mansuben,* and they were primarily preoccupied with studying the moves of the endgame that would lead to check and the winning of the game. All chess pieces were of equal importance and ways of solving endgame problems were clearly defined. There were constant bids of check and it was usual to sacrifice many pieces. However, we should not be led to false conclusions by these documents. The nobility and upper middle classes played thousands of games purely for pleasure, as an enjoyable pastime. The classic literature of the day did not always accurately reflect the tedious monotony of daily life.

Chess was regarded as a true reflection of class-based society. A pamphlet written about 1275 by Jacobo da Cessole, an Italian Dominican monk, is characteristic of this medieval opinion. The pamphlet was titled *Liber de moribus Hominum et officiis nobilium ac Popularium super ludo scaccorum* (Chess Book on the Morals of Mankind and the Duties of the Nobility and Lower Classes). Soon, 200 handwritten copies of the pamphlet were being read all over Europe. Cessole inter-

Este es otro iuego departido en q̃ a x.
trebeios que an a seer entablados aſi
como eſta en la figura del entabla-
mieto.τ an ſe de iogar ceſta gui-
ſa. los puetos ui ſa...
egan pmero τ dan ma-
te al rey blanco en q̃-
tro uezes o en menos
delos ſus iuegos miſ-
mos ſi los blancos no
lo ſopieren alongar. ❡ El pumero
iuego dar la raque con el peon pueto en la tercera caſa del cauallo blan-
co.τ iogara el rey blanco en la caſa de
ſo cauallo. τ ſi entraſſe en caſa de ſo
roque. ſerie mate a la pumera uez
con el roque pueto en la caſa del cauallo blanco. ❡ El ſegundo iuego
dar la raque con el roque pueto en
la caſa del cauallo blanco.τ encobri-
ra el rey blanco con ſo alfil. ❡ El t-
cero iuego dar la raque con el roq̃
pueto que eſta en ſu caſa poniendol
en la caſa del roque blanco.τ el rey

blanco tomar loa por fuerça. ❡ El
quarto iuego dar la raque mathe
con el roque pueto tomando el alfil blanco que eſta en ſu caſa. ❡ E ſi
los puetos entaren de dar raque cada
uez al rey blanco. es el rey pueto τ
mathe al pumero iuego con el roq̃
blanco poniendol en la ſegunda caſa del alfil pueto. ❡ Eſte es el de-
partimiento deſte iuego. τ eſta es la
figura dell entablamiento.

The Dominican monk, Jacobo da Cessole, who, in 1275, wrote the most-copied chess book of the Middle Ages. After the invention of printing, his work appeared in many further editions. This page is of such an edition from 1413 with the picture of Cessole.

Below right: *"The wise men or bishops of the game were portrayed as judges or advisers, sitting with an open book,"* (from the Cessole Codex, Bibliotheca Vaticana).

Opposite: *Jacobo da Cessole preaching a sermon. In a period when chess was extremely popular, he used the game to cloak his sermons on vice and virtue.*

preted chess figures in the light of the social order prevalent in this period. Chess was also an integral part of court life. Troubadours sang its praises, and many priests were enthusiastic players. Hugo von Trimberg, who lived near Bamberg, wrote in 1300: "This world resembles a chessboard. Both are peopled with kings, queens, counts (rooks), knights, judges (bishops) and peasants (pawns). If we study this matter seriously we can see that God leads us through His game in the same way as a player moves his chess figures. The man who sur-

renders to sinful thoughts will always be held in check by the devil and will lose his soul to mate if he does not know how to protect himself." Chess, in the opinion of Hugo von Trimberg, reflected the divine order of the world.

The transition to a faster moving form of chess occurred at the end of the 15th century. This development was characterized by longer moves over more than two

oltoru
fratrū
ordiꝰ
vꝛi et diuersoꝝ
ſeularū precibus
pſwaſuꝰ dudum
munuꝰ reqſitum
nectaui videlicet
reiſinꝰ morum
ac belli ſumani
ꝉ generiꝰ docum̄tꝰ
Sane tu illum ad
pꝑlm declamatoie
pꝑdicaſſem multiꝰ
ꝗ nobilibuꝰ placuiſſet materia honori eoꝝ
at dictati aſcribere monenꝰ eoꝰ ut ſi foꝛaꝰ
eoꝝ menti ipꝛeſſerit libellum ipꝱm et ludi
virtutem corde faciliter poterunt obtinere
ſunt etiam libellum de moꝛibuꝰ hōm et de
officiꝰ nobiliū intitulare decreui et ut ordi
naciꝰ pꝛedam m eo an ipꝱm capla lectoꝛi
pꝑoſui ut ꝗ in eo ſequitur clariuꝰ elicceſtat
Tractatibuꝰ aut quatuoꝛ opuꝰ ipꝱm lectoꝛ
nouit eſſe diſtinctum. Pꝛimuꝰ tractatuꝰ de
cauſa inuencionꝰ huꝰ ludi ꝉmꝰ caꝮm ſub quo
rege ſit hic ludꝰ inuentuꝰ e 2ꝰm quiꝰ ludum
inueit 3ꝰm de triplici cauſa inuencionꝰ hꝰ

curaui

cuiuſ

BIBLIOTHECA APOSTOLICA VATICANA

squares by the *fers* (queen) and *fil* (bishop). Chess competitions gradually began to take place. In 1467, the first recorded chess tournament in Central Europe was held in Heidelberg, organized by the *"Schachzabelspiel"* Society.

Throughout its history, chess has not been the prerogative of experts. It was also played by begin-

captured as many pieces as possible and gave check as many times as possible. The discovery of printing played a decisive role in the rapid development and conformity of chess rules. Cessole's booklet was printed in 1473, followed by editions translated into many European languages. William Caxton, an English chess enthusiast and printer, used a

Paul Murphy (1837 – 1884) was a brilliant American player who, as Philidor had done before him, brought the chess world to its feet with his blindfold simultaneous exhibitions. In the Café de la Régence in 1858, he won 6 out of 8 games. Illustration in Harper's Weekly, *November, 1858.*

ners and became a part of social gatherings. Both levels of players would have registered in this first tournament so, of course, we cannot expect that the standard of play would have reached our present level of defined openings, positional play, well-thought-out strategy and endgame technique. The game was primarily battle in which players

French translation of this work as the basis for his book published in Bruges. This was the first chess book in English, *The Game and Play of Chess*. The first German translation was printed in Augsburg in 1477. Cessole's book proved to be very popular; there were about 70 copies in Latin, 40 in German, 20 in French and ten in Italian. The very

> "One attempts to disprove the erroneous opinion
> that each move must have an immediate effect;
> even waiting and resting moves
> have a reason for existence."
>
> *Aaron Nimzowitsch*

first printed chess book, *Das Guldin Spiel,* was published in Augsburg in 1472 by Gunter Zainer, only 16 years after Gutenberg had invented the printing press. The author was a certain Master Ingold. The numerous books printed in this short period of time show just how popular chess had become in Europe by the end of the Middle Ages. In players, blindfolded players who amazed both nonplayers and experts alike, chess books with detailed analyses of playing systems, collections of games and an interested public. The first European book giving instructions on how to play chess, a book that still meets modern requirements, was written by the Spanish player Luis Ramirez

> "I believe that chess possesses a magic that is also of help in advanced age. A rheumatic knee is forgotten during a game of chess and other events can seem quite unimportant in comparison with a catastrophe on the chess-board. A visit to a chess club keeps one young and, in particular, contact with the younger generation can give new impetus."
>
> *Vlastimil Hort in "Chess is life"*

the 16th century castling, in a similar form to that of today, was adopted in Italy and Spain — *i.e.,* squares that could be put in check could no longer be moved over. By the beginning of the 17th century, chess had all the characteristics of modern world chess: professional players, international competitions, team competitions, glorified star de Lucena. Published in 1497, it carried the title *Repetición de amores e arte de axedres* and listed the opening moves used at that time, plus 150 problems, and the old and new chess rules.

In 1891, the Polish-French chess champion, Samuel Rosenthal (1837 – 1902), played a simultaneous game in Paris on 30 boards which, at that time, was considered an incredible performance. Contemporary illustration.

L'ANALYZE DES ECHECS: Contenant Une Nouvelle Methode Pour apprendre en peu de tems à fe Perfectioner dans ce NOBLE JEU. Par A. D. PHILIDOR.

Ludimus Effigie Belli. VIDA.

A LONDRES, L'An MDCCXLIX.

THE FIRST PROFESSIONAL PLAYERS

Right: Title page of the first edition of Philidor's famous Book on Chess, published 1749 in French language in London.

Below center: Charles the Bold, Duke of Burgundy (1433–1477), invited famous chess players to his court to display their talents. The players were given a princely reward.

Below right: Philip II, King of Spain (1527 to 1598), depicted here at age 59, sponsored the first international tournament between Italians and Spaniards.

Spain and Italy were the first centers of European chess. Both countries produced renowned chess masters, organized the first international tournaments and dominated the chess scene well into the 18th century. Expert practical advice on how to gain an advantage in a game. "If you are playing by daylight, always seat yourself so that the sun will shine into your opponent's eyes. This will give you a definite advantage. In addition, try to arrange that you

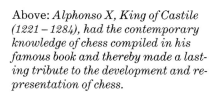

Above: Alphonso X, King of Castile (1221–1284), had the contemporary knowledge of chess compiled in his famous book and thereby made a lasting tribute to the development and representation of chess.

players from both centuries moved from court to court and from one town to another, seldom meeting opponents who could play at their level. Lucena's book had already implied that competitive games had become battles for prestige, and that playing ability alone did not always decide the winner. He gave

play after your opponent had had a large meal and a lot to drink." It is not surprising that similar tactics are still practiced by modern grand masters to try to disturb their opponent's concentration. The Brazilian grand master Henrique Mecking accused Tigran Petrosyan, World Champion from 1963–69, of only sitting still when it was his own turn to play. "While I was considering my move he kept kicking the table and pushing his elbows down on the table until the board shook. As if that was not bad enough, he kept making noises, stirring his coffee in ever-changing rhythms, and rolling a coin across the table." When Mecking tried to play him back in kind, he found himself outmaneuvered. Petrosyan was hard of hearing and simply turned off his hearing aid. He also won the game.

Chess was keenly fostered in the royal courts of Europe. Both Charles, Duke of Orleans (1391 to 1465), himself a good player, and Charles the Bold, Duke of Burgundy (1433 – 1477), attracted many well-known chess players to their courts. In Italy, the Duke of Seram, Giacomo Buoncampagno (1538 – 1612), encouraged both the game and its players. In 1575, the first Spanish International Tournament was held at the court of King Philip II. The famous Italian masters, Leonardo da Cutro and Paola Boi, seconded by Guilo Cesare Polerio, defeated the great Spanish masters Ruy Lopez and Alfonso Ceron. The expert players and their playing systems now began to dominate public awareness. They provided a standard for excellence; if anyone wanted to win fame as a player, he first had to defeat the famous masters of Italy, Spain, Portugal, France and England. A player's fame was often equaled by the jealousy he aroused. Leonardo da Cutro is thought to have been poisoned by those who envied him.

Charles, Duke of Orleans (1391 to 1465), was a keen chess enthusiast. He was popularly called "the chess-player." He played against famous Italian players.

Success ensured generous prize money. Early in the 17th century, the Duke of Lorraine rewarded chess master Gioacchino Greco (ca. 1600 – 1634), a student of Polerio, with the sum of 5,000 scudi for his performance at the court, a fortune even by today's standards. A year later Greco defeated the English masters. His magnificent combinational games are still well-known and have passed into tournament practice. For Greco, chess was both an art and a science. He perceived subtleties in the game that can safely be placed on a level with abstract mathematics. The working relationships he discovered and introduced into positional play possessed fine ramifications which are only now becoming generally understood. The tradition of the Italian masters ended with Domenico Ponziani (1719 – 1796). His game was representative of the once highly acclaimed school of Modena. Ponziani and Giambattista Lolli (1698 – 1769) published important chess analyses which led to a higher level of perfection in the endgame and which strengthened an open-board game out of the opening.

A new era in the "Game of Kings" was ushered in by the Frenchman François-André Danican Philidor (1726 – 1795). Following his victories in 1747 in Slaught-

The German Adolf Anderssen (1818 to 1879) won the famous London Tournament in 1851 and was, therefore, the first unofficial World Champion. He was a superb attacker.

DIDEROT

The founder of the Encyclopaedia, *the great Diderot, greatly admired Philidor but warned him against the mental exertion required for his simultaneous blindfold games. He feared that Philidor would lose his reason.*

In England, some of the well-known chess players of the 19th century: János Jakob Löwenthal (1810 – 1875), Jules Arnoux de Rivière (1830 to 1905), Marmaduke Wyvill (1814 to 1896), Ernst Karl Falkbeer (1819 to 1885), Howard Staunton (1810 to 1874), Lyttelton and H. A. Kennedy.

er's Coffee House in London against the Syrian master, Phillip Stamma, and in 1750 against Sire Kermur de Légal, he was acknowledged as the greatest player of his time. His fame made London and Paris the new centers of the chess world. When he announced that he would publish an instructional book, *L'Analyze du Jeu des Echecs,* the subscription list included the most famous names in London society. In 1751, he demonstrated his amazing mastery of chess in Potsdam and in Berlin where he played before Frederick the Great. All of London praised his simultaneous per-

of 14, he played chess in the famous meeting place of chess enthusiasts, the Café de la Régence in Paris. Later he played many games there against Rousseau, d'Alembert, Diderot and Robespierre, and the Café became the center of the chess world. After his victory over Légal, Philidor's friends presented him with a scepter as a symbol of his unique mastery of chess. Both directly and indirectly, Philidor's teachings led to the rise of the national chess schools in Europe. Howard Staunton (1810 – 1874) published both the first English chess magazine *The Chess Player's Chronicle* in 1841,

formances blindfolded and the whole world was at his feet. His famous contemporary Denis Diderot, philosopher and co-founder of the *L'Encyclopédie,* specifically warned him against such strenuous mental exertion fearing that he would lose his reason. Philidor was more methodical than Greco. He discovered the value of the pawns and always aimed at building a strong center. Philidor had first attracted attention when, at the age

and the first English chess handbook in 1847. In addition, in 1851 he organized the first international chess tournament to be held in London. The first handbook in Russian was written in 1824 by Alexander Petroj (1794 – 1867), who went on to become one of the founders of the Russian school. Even at a later date, Philidor's influence was still making itself felt in Paris. In the Café de la Régence four renowned players followed in his footsteps – La Bourdonnais, Saint-Amant, Deschapelles and the Livonian-born Kieseritzky. Up until 1840, the Café was so crowded with players and onlookers that people kept their hats on to save space.

In 1803, the first chess club that could boast its own premises was founded in Berlin. Here again, Philidor was the shining light. This chess society, which was soon regularly visited by famous players from as far afield as London, Budapest and St. Petersburg, produced Paul Rudolf von Bilguer (1815–1840), the author of the first German chess book which also gained recognition outside Germany. In addition, he founded the first German chess periodical, known since 1846 as the *Deutsche Schachzeitung,* the world's oldest chess newspaper still in publication.

Adolf Anderssen (1818–1879) was a professor of mathematics and the German language. The Berlin "Chess Society" sponsored his entry in the first London International Tournament. Anderssen caused a sensation when he became the undisputed victor, defeating Kieseritzky, Szen, Staunton, who had been the favorite, and Wyrill. This was the beginning of a new era in chess history. New, higher standards were set. From then on, chess developed into a game of grand champions. Players made thorough studies of opponents' moves and of chess theory: both became basic requirements for success at the highest level, of international competition. The first official World Champion, Wilhelm Steinitz, crushed opponents with superior strategy and breath taking tactics. From this period on, the requirements for success were analytical thinking, concentrated study, intellectual and physical fitness, mental tenacity, an intuitive grasp of difficult positions, creative combinational play and a computer-like memory.

CHESS — MIRROR OF THE UNIVERSE

Chess can no longer be regarded as a simple game. Even though at lower and middle levels of play it is still a social pastime, in tournaments the game is a test of strength and a witness to the human spirit. It mirrors the history of civilization in just as classical a manner as does political history. Human nature is reflected in both; depth of thought, cunning ruses, patient defence, boisterous spirits, keen aggression, tactical fitness and the issue to win as well as our tragic flaws, our unability to accept our weakness and defeat.

The ancient Indian chess game was a game of war and had no aim other than to imitate, on a board, the real events on a battlefield. However, chess was soon felt to be something more. The Indians themselves, and then the Persians and Arabs, had raised it, through a great deal of concentration and combined thinking, to a serious, in-

"I know of no spectacle on earth that can keep 3,000 people enthralled for five hours. Utterly immobile and deep in thought, the players sit facing each other like the hieratic actors in a Japanese Kabuki production."

Fernando Arrabal on the Moscow championships

Right: *Two wood carvings pictured in one of the oldest English chess books, Caxton's* Game and Playe of the Chesse, *from the year 1474. On the left a monk is trying to solve a chess problem, and on the right a game is taking place between a king and a bishop.*

tellectual game. This peaceful contest was aimed at denouncing war and destruction in the minds of mankind. As such, it reflected the Buddhist religion and the ancient wisdom of India. The dimension of space was captured on the chessboard by the squares and the figures representing the weapons of human warfare, the soldiers, cavalry,

The Garden of Love. A copperplate etching by the German Master E. S. showing a couple playing chess. Circa 1445 – 50.

elephants and chariots. The dimension of time was made real by the continuing movements on the board. Every move changed the overall position just as time changed the lives and destinies of rulers and their subjects. The Arabian historian Masudi, who died in Cairo in 958, perceived similarities between chess and the movements of the

heavenly bodies. The idea of chess as a mirror of the universe is still alive today. "Chess is the world, the playing pieces are what we see in space, and the game rules are the natural laws," wrote the British naturalist Thomas Huxley. The philosopher, Rudolf Steiner, also thought that chess mirrored the scheme of the universe.

In the courts of the Middle Ages, chess was not aligned with eternity. An evocative French poem "Les échecs amoureux" (ca. 1400) likened the game of love to chess. A favorite theme of paintings was couples playing chess in stylized romantic groves. Lovers were portrayed playing the game in brightly-colored, open-air settings reminiscent of Paradise. Priceless chessboards and chessmen are evidence that the aristocracy were keen players, but many churchmen were also enthusiasts. The Benedictine monks, the most important religious order in the Western world, held chess in high regard as a mental discipline, on a par with mathematics. The Dominican monk Jacobo da Cessole saw in chess an allegory of social order. His writings describe the chess figures as having their counterparts in the real medieval world. Moralizing pamphlets were happy to expand this theme. Our own century has produced its own share of unusual interpretations of chess figures. Reuben Fine, an

American grand master, and one of the eight greatest chess players between 1930 and 1940, wrote his *Psychology of Chess Players* in 1956, a book which was reissued in 1967. Fine, who was also a successful psychoanalyst, propounded the theory that homosexual and aggressive tendencies were sublimated in chess. The king, a phallic symbol, was accompanied or followed by a castration complex. Checkmate represented castration or patricide, and the pawns symbolized children, usually young boys.

Although chess has its origins in the Indian world and had been adopted and spread by the Persian-Arabian world, both great religions of these nations were openly hostile to games of any kind. Buddha condemned all games as idle and vain because they distracted his followers from the more difficult struggle of the search for truth. Mohammed also denounced games as being sinful, but as the Prophet had not specifically mentioned chess (probably because he had never heard of it), its Arab adherents decided that he could not possibly have meant chess. The devout holy man Ibn Dawud believed that chess players deserved the strongest condemnation, and Habba, an Arabian zealot, proclaimed, "Chess is cursed and so is anyone who plays it." This denunciation is reminiscent of the ascetic stand taken by the Cister-

cian monks in Europe during the Middle Ages, for they also condemned the game. In the 13th century, the church imposed several bans on the game. However, many eloquent and noble interpretations of the game by ingenious chess advocates eventually overcame these religiously motivated attacks.

In the foreword to Alfonso X's chess book we read, "God wants his children to enjoy all kinds of entertainment so that they will be able to tolerate the worries and troubles that may beset them." The son of a caliph, who considered himself the successor to the Prophet, defended chess against all its detractors in his timeless verses:
You, with your cynical mockery
Criticize our beloved chess,
Know that skill is here a science,
That the game disperses sadness.
It eases the lover's heartache,
Protects the drinker from excess,
And gives advice to the warrior
When danger nears and destruction threatens.
When our need is greatest, it provides a companion in our loneliness.

Dances of Death and games with death were widespread at the end of the Middle Ages. Wall frescoes and paintings on panels were often found in the churches. "The Game of Death" is a fresco by Albertus Pictor found in the church in Täby, Sweden (second half of the 15th century).

Title page of the first edition of the Polish poem "Chess" by Jan Kodanowski which was published in 1564.

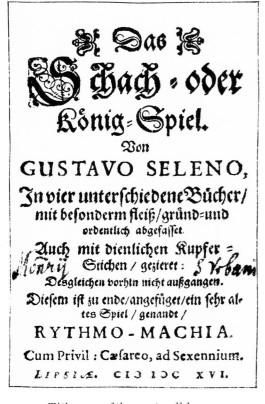

Title page of the most well-known German chess book. It was written by Gustavus Selenus, a pseudonym used by Duke August of Braunschweig and Lüneburg (1579 – 1666) to conceal his real identity. It appeared in 1616.

Right: *The game known as Astronomy Chess is played on a round board. The firmament, the planets, and the signs of the zodiac were the main elements.*

FAME TO THE NATIONS — HONOR TO THE PLAYERS

The game was refined by many national schools of chess and their outstanding players. Chess literature refers to, among others, the Indian, Spanish, Scottish and Viennese Systems; the French, Scandinavian, Dutch, Hungarian, Russian, Sicilian and Polish defences; the Catalonian Opening; the Latvian Gambit; and the Czechoslovakian System of the Slovakian Defence.

This never-ending variety in Grand Championship Chess is maybe what Masudi was hinting at in the ancient Persian legend of the grains of corn, a legend that told of the origin of chess. In India, in the reign of King Balhit about 120 years after King Poros had been conquered by Alexander the Great, the legend tells of an Indian vizier who invented chess. As his only reward for this notable achievement, he asked the king for grains of corn. The quantity was to be calculated in the following manner: for the first of the 64 chess squares he asked for one grain of corn; for the second square, two grains; for the third, four grains; for the fourth, eight grains, and so on. The initial astonishment of the king and his court soon turned to consternation as the

calculations showed that the last square, the 64th, would require 9,223,372,036,854,775,808 grains of corn, and that the grand total for the whole board would be 18,446,744,073,709,551,615 grains. All of India would not have been large enough to harvest such a volume.

There is a lot to be learned from this legend. The decimal system was discovered in India and the basis for the logarithmic system is also found in this legend. The diversity of chess attracted great mathematicians to uncover certain laws. The mathematician Leonard Euler from Basle, examined the inherent possibilities of the knight's move, and in Germany the mathematician and as-

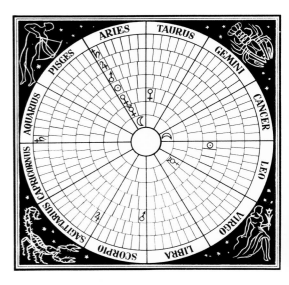

tronomer Karl Friedrich Gauss occupied himself with finding positions for eight queens from which they could not attack each other. He discovered 82 possible positions. Such exercises clearly demonstrate the incredible diversity of chess. There are 3,612 ways of placing two

1	2	4	8	16	32	64	128
256	512	1024	2048	4096	8192	16384	32768
65536	131072	262144	524288	1048576	2097152	4194304	8388608
16777216	33554432	67108864	134217728	268435456	536870912	1073741824	2147483648
4294967296	8589934592	17179869184	34359738368	68719476736	137438953472	274877906944	549755813888
1099511627776	2199023255552	4398046511104	8796093022208	17592186044416	35184372088832	70368744177664	140737488355328
281474976710656	562949953421312	1125899906842624	2251799813685248	4503599627370496	9007199254740992	18014398509481984	36028797018963968
72057594037927936	144115188075855872	288230376151711744	576460752303423488	1152921504606846976	2305843009213693952	4611686018427387904	9223372036854775808

= 18 446 744 073 709 551 615

kings on the board; two kings and two pawns can be placed in 7.4 million correct game positions; two kings and two bishops can produce a total of 13 million positions. The complete set of 32 pieces can be positioned in combinations that produce a number of 117 digits. Even if a few digits are deducted because some positions could never actually be used, the exercise serves the purpose of illustrating the great number of potential positions. Of course, it is not theoretically possible to use this great range of positions in a single game of chess, but, in human terms, chess is a world of its own.

The greatest lasting honor for a chess player, other than carrying off the World Championship title, is to have his name associated with an opening, a gambit, a defence, a variation or a trap. A few examples are listed here to illustrate the diversity of chess: the Staunton Gambit (named after the British chess master who was recognized as the greatest player in the world between 1843 and 1851); the Caro-Kann Defence (named after the Anglo-German player Horatio Caro (1862 – 1920), and the Viennese Marcus Kann, who died in 1886; the Cunningham Gambit (after the British Ambassador in Venice (1715 to 1720), who analyzed a variation in the King's Gambit); the Falkbeer Counter-Gambit (in honor of the Austrian master who played around 1850); the Jaenisch Gambit (analyzed in 1847 by the co-founder of the Russian chess school); the Marshall Attack (a clever variation

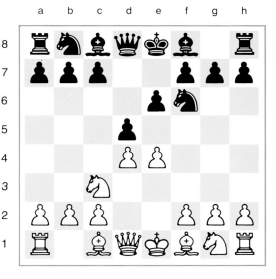

The classic strategy of the French Defense:
1.e4 e6 2.d4 d5 3.Nc3 Nf6

The French Defense was one of the oldest and, for a long time, one of the most popular. It was adopted by many theoreticians such as Alapin as an attack strategy for Black. There are many variations of this defense.

"Sacrifices are only possible
when one's opponent has made a mistake."
"It is always better
to sacrifice the opponent's pieces."

Savielly Tartakover

on the Spanish System that was first played in New York in 1918 by the American grand master against Capablanca); the Max Lange Attack (first executed by the German master and problem theorist in the middle of the 19th century); the Muzio Gambit (a variation on the King's Gambit wrongly credited in 1634 to the Neapolitan Muzio d'Alessandro); the Nimzowitsch Defence, known since the 16th century and played in 1907 at Ostende on the Baltic by one of the best players in the world between 1925 and 1930); the Réti Opening, introduced into tournament games in 1923 by

against Marshall); the Englund Gambit (first played by this Swedish master, 1871–1933); the Botvinnik Variation of the Slav Combination (named after the three-time Russian World Champion, who, at the age of 50, won the World Championship title for the third time); the Canal Trap (in honor of the Peruvian International Master Estebán Canal, who died in 1981, for his discovery of an opening trap in the Italian Game).

Equally deserving of immortality is the "Immortal Game," played in 1851 by Adolf Anderssen against Lionel Kieseritzky; the "Evergreen

Below center:
The Rubinstein variation:
1.e4 e6 2.d4 d5 3.Nc3 dxe4

Below right: The Tarrasch variation:
1.e4 e6 2.d4 d5 3.Nd2 ...

Above: The Nimzowitsch variation:
1.e4 e6 2.d4 d5 3.Nc3 Bb4

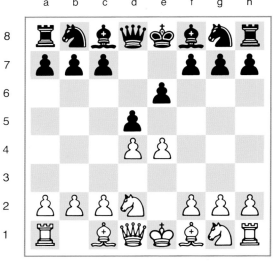

the Czechoslovakian grand master and founder of the "Hypermoderne Schachschule"; the Alekhine variation (first used in the contest in 1934 between the Russian World Master and Bogoljubov); the Tarrasch Defence (often played in the Queen's Gambit declined by the German master after 1880); the Winawer Counter-Gambit (named after the Polish master who first used it in Monte Carlo in 1901

Game," also played successfully by Anderssen in 1853 in a friendly game against Jean Dufresne, a master from Berlin and author of books teaching chess; and the "Immortal *Zugzwang* Game," first made world famous when it was used in a contest between Friedrich Saemisch, the first German international master after the Second World War, and Nimzowitsch. Saemisch, with White and a full board,

> "The last mistake wins.
> The threat is more effective
> than the actual implementation."
>
> *Savielly Tartakover*

was forced into *Zugzwang* and, after only 25 moves, had to concede defeat. Equally famous is the "Immortal Problem," thought out by the Austrian problem specialist Konrad Bayer, 1828–1897. World acclaim was also earned by Akiba Rubinstein (1882–1961), the great Polish grand master and one of the best players in the world between 1907 and 1914, for his inspired endgame combination known as "Rubinstein's Immortal." A series of moves known as the "Steinitz Jewel" in honor of world champion Wilhelm Steinitz, who first used it at the age of 80, is still admired.

castled position of the black king. "Légal's Mate" is named in memory of Sire Kermur de Légal, who in 1750 placed Saint-Briee in mate in only seven moves. In Germany, this move is known as the Sea-Cadet Mate.

The person who occupies himself with the study of chess does so with the purpose of increasing his understanding of the game. Whoever studies the history of mankind will more than likely become a pessimist whereas the serious student of chess will also become a better player. Chess strategy and theory as understood today have been so thoroughly

Below left: The Marshall variation:
1.e4 e6 2.d4 d5 3.Nc3 c5

Below center: The Alapin variation:
1.e4 e6 2.d4 d5 3.Be3 …

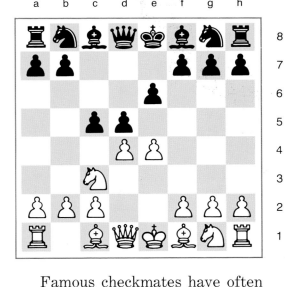

Famous checkmates have often been given the names of successful victors. This rare honor shows respect for those names who made chess history. "Greco's Mate" made its way into chess history after a confrontation in 1916. In this game, Gioacchino Greco, the never-to-beforgotten Italian chess master of the 17th century, sacrificed his bishop and carried through a wonderful combination against the

analyzed that an almost fail safe system has evolved with clear definitions of good and bad moves. It would therefore be easy to assume that the player who makes the correct moves will win the game, but this is not so. The victor will be the player who, at a crucial point in the game, can confidently move his chessmen in such a way that he can avoid making a move which will give his opponent the advantage.

Above: The Cchigorin variation:
1.e4 e6 2.Qe2 …

"The Chess Game." A painting by the Dutch artist Lucas van Leyden from the year 1508.

"The Middle Ages did not content itself with mere externals: the immediate and the usual always had to mean something distant and more important and only the outermost envelope of a deeper-seated meaning."

> "Chess possesses a wonderful quality: it concentrates one's mental energy on one narrow area, so that the brain isn't worn out by the most strenuous effort of thought.
> Its agility and vigour are actually improved."
>
> *Stefan Zweig*
> *in "The Royal Game"*

THE ESSENCE OF THE GAME

Miniature and text from the manuscript written by Jacobo da Cessole (1407). Bavarian State Library, Munich.
"The Queen must be presented as a beautiful woman, draped in a gold robe bordered with fur and she should stand to her left of the chess board so that she can embrace the king in her right hand."

Opposite: *Mephisto playing chess for Dr. Faust's soul. A painted clock from around 1900. The clock mechanism moves the Devil's eyes.*

Chess is beautiful and difficult. Indeed, its beauty is revealed precisely in its difficulties. Chess has two faces. One face displays the charm of the geometric chess pieces with their noble proportions, pure form and clearcut lines. Here, strictness and sharpness of intellect reign, yet there is also lightness and serenity. The other face bears wild and fantastic, sometimes even secretive and demonic images. They reflect the beauty of movement, adventure and danger. Everyone who plays chess with an open heart and mind is addicted to both faces.

In other areas, the chess fan is similarly familiar with pairs of concepts that clearly show the inner richness of the game. In all good games, strategy and tactic are considered and positional requirements and combination possibilities are weighed. Strategy means planning for a long term goal which requires a mind capable of computing smoothly as well as recognizing opportunities and dangers. A tactic is an aimed blow, a calculated assault, a well-constructed defense. Those who think strategically but ignore tactics have their heads in the clouds; on the other hand, those who merely play tactics and neglect the over all picture chase their own tails. It has become common knowledge that the attack, the darling of the beginner, must be warranted by the position; that combinations, especially the brilliant ones, demand a solid position. It is true that some grand masters are classified as combinational players, others as posi-

tional players. That means that each player has his strong points, but those strengths are not enough. A combination calls for precision and imagination; the essential assessment of position requires reason and intuition, logic and instinct. A chess ancient, eternally youthful game or is it slowly dying out? Haven't all possibilities been exhausted by now? Definitely not. Hardly ever have two serious games been identical. Although countless sequences of moves have been recorded, the desire to invent new ones remains undiminished. Thousands of games have been precisely analyzed, yet new ideas and inspirations are constantly applied on the board.

It is this inexhaustibility of ideas that brings the game so near to art. With many other games whose rules are similarly strict, the possibilities for gaining advantages are limited from the start. This is not the case in chess, which is not confined and repetitious. In showing great admiration, one speaks of "creative chess." Yet, despite its art and creativity, today there are players and officials who want to put chess in a class next to sports. That makes sense as far as the affiliation of chess associations to a parent organization, government subsidies for competition or the placement of instructional diagrams and notations in daily newspapers. However, for all its competitive nature, chess is not a typical sport. The intellectual exertions of chess players cannot be compared with the physical exertions of athelets. Some masters may feel as tired after a game as they would if they had run a long distance race and some players may lose ten pounds during a tournament. However, simple observation or common sense should convince a

The tracks of a famous game. Bobby Fischer was 13 years old when, playing with black, he competed against Donal Byrne, and by sacrificing his queen proved that he was more than just a promising talent. Artist Ugo Dossi traced the path of every chess piece in a color corresponding to that of its starting square – red for the king, green for the knight etc.

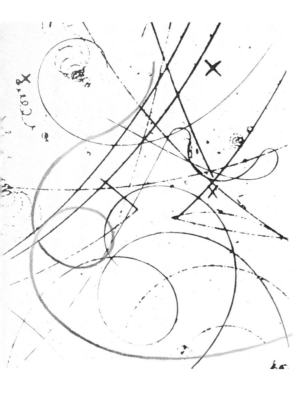

reasonable person that someone who sits and thinks is not participating in a sport, but in mental acrobatics at most. The term "science" is used in most chess books. Indeed, an independent methodology has been developed for the study of openings, mid-game and endgame play, as well as strategy and tactics. However, despite all the theory, chess remains a practical affair. It is simply a game sui generis, indiosyncratic, unique, unmistakable. Who tends to take up this game? There is no definitive answer to that question. A pre-requisite for becoming a good chess player, however, is a mind that can subject itself to a certain discipline, yet also come up with original ideas. Steady nerves are desirable, but not, as many believe, all important from the outset. The ambitious player certainly has enough time to train and steel his nerves during play.

Every chess player counts and calculates. He counts the squares to find out if his king can catch his opponent's pawn before it is queened. The player calculates variations, for which he retains ten or twenty factors in his memory and must observe their sequence precisely. The chessboard's geometry, the logic of the rules of play, and, indeed, abstract reasoning, as well as the concepts "right" and "wrong" are reminiscent of mathematics. Indeed, the gallery of great players includes several mathematicians, such as Wilhelm Steinitz, who officially became world champion in 1866, Emanuel Lasker, world champion in 1894, and Max Euwe, world champion in 1935. Adolph Anderssen, one of the best players of the 19th century, taught mathematics at a high school in Breslau, and Richard Réti, the great theorist of the 20th century, had at least started to study mathematics. Michail Botvinnik, who won the world championship in 1948, and Milan Vidmar, a Yugoslavian grand master and charming storyteller were engineers. On the other hand, some chess masters never studied algebra or geometry, but could still count squares and figure out variations. Siegbert Tarrasch, Lasker's adversary, was a doctor in Nuremberg, and Reuben Fine, a star of the 1930s, was a psychiatrist in New York. The ranks also included businessmen such as Louis Paulsen in the 19th century and Miguel Najdorf in the 20th century. Howard Staunton, the godfather of today's typical, standardized chessmen ac-

Left: *The moves made by the knight in graphic from as in the picture on the left? No. This is an illustration of the passage of an accelerated subatomic particle through a fog chamber. Ugo Dossi worked out a formal analogy between chess and nuclear physics. The chess enthusiast considers this a compliment and out of politeness refrains from asking if worse games don't create a similar impression on the eye as the Byrne-Fischer masterpiece.*

"I was four years old when I got my first intimation of what chess is. My father often played in the evenings with one or other of his friends. I was present and absorbedly played whole battles with the defeated pieces. Some time later, my father taught me the rules and chess became more than a toy to me. He played serious games with me and did not spare my pride. After losing, I always wanted to burst into tears, but he warned me: 'Without loss, there can be no victories. But if you cry, I won't play with you any more. That has been a lesson to me all my life'."

Anatoly Karpov in "Chess" 1984

tually designed by Nathaniel Cook, became a Shakespeare scholar. Before becoming prominent chess players at the beginning of the century, Efim Bogolyubov studied theology and Akiba Rubinstein wanted to be a rabbi. Alexander Alekhine, who became world champion in 1927, studied law and could have joined a profession that Euwe, a mathematician, apparently viewed as eminently fitting for a chess player: "As a lawyer, he knew how to defend even a bad affair well." That observation was especially aimed at the lawyer Savielly

Tartakover. But every exceptional player has been skilled in holding weak positions by means of all sorts of ruses and tricks. Alekhine's predecessor, José Raúl Capablanca, world champion in 1921, was a bona fide playboy. Capablanca fits into a glorious tradition of passionate devotion to chess. Over and over again, people who could and wanted to do virtually nothing but play chess have been a topic of conversa-

tion. One of them was Joseph Henry Blackburne, who at the turn of the century claimed that he had played 50,000 games of chess in his life, which was to last another two decades. Blackburne, who sported a black beard as well as his "black" name and at times won furiously playing the unfavored black pieces, was called "the black death." Showing his lighter side, the black Englishman once quipped: "Personally, alcohol helps me to keep a clear head." In any case, neither Steinitz nor Lasker lost to Blackburne.

After World War II, almost all outstanding masters were professional chess players. The fact that Vasily Smyslov, world champion in 1957, was said to have also wanted to become an opera singer, attracted unusual attention. Some professional players today hold doctoral degrees: John Nunn in mathematics and Robert Hübner in classical philology. The world champions following Smyslov – Mikail Tal (1960), Tigran Petrosyan (1963), Boris Spassky (1969), Robert Fischer (1972), Anatoly Karpov (1975) and Garry Kasparov (1985) havn't though of any other profession but that of chess player. Johannes Hermann Zukertort certainly had a more varied life. He was a linguist, doctor, pianist, sharpshooter, political journalist and, for all that, the rival of world champion Steinitz at the chessboard.

THE ROYAL GAME

A good king was king for all his subjects; the old and the young, the rich and the poor, the city and the country dwellers. Similarly, the royal game exists for everyone. It does not cost much to play. An oilcloth board and a set of chess pieces suffice; some sort of table and two chairs are easily obtainable. Formerly, the game was usually played for money, and someone who won a lot of money at chess could easily have entertained the odd idea of making this pleasure his business. However, professional players, such as Carl Schlechter, lived from hand to mouth. Schlechter, an Austrian hopeful for the world chess championship, died of starvation in 1918. Today, in Russia

Wie der meister verßes von dem ersten leret
Das schossßabel spil spilen In des kunges hoff ritter
vnd knechte vnd wie der kung dar zu kam gegange

> "A chess game can only be won when the balance is lost. In a position with perfect balance, even the greatest genius is helpless – the position offers no inspiration!"

Wilhelm Steinitz

An artist of the late Middle Ages, possibly Hans Schilling, captured in this colored pen and ink picture of King Evilmerodach the moment at which someone is overwhelmed by his love for chess. The miniature is taken from Konrad von Ammenhausen's chess book from 1467.

and many European countries, large prizes at tournaments and lucrative positions for teachers make it possible for chess masters to make a good living. The best players may even become millionaires, but in the United States only a handful of masters eke out a living at the game.

Chess players mature slowly. Most of them exhibit their greatest performances between 30 and 40 years of age. Before that time, they lack experience and judgement: after that they begin to lose stamina and concentration. An example is Tigran Petrosyan, who lost his World Championship title exactly on his 40th birthday. However, there are many exceptions. Mikail Tal reached his peak at the early age of 23; Garry Kasparov reached his even earlier, at 22. Usually, though, the performance curve resembles an elongated, arched cat's back. The game is suitable for children as well as the elderly, for impetuous youth and mellowed adults. In chess, as in mathematics and music, child prodigies perform up to adult

standards. Arturo Pomar, a Spaniard, was heralded as a whiz kid after
defeating Saemisch at 11 years of
age in 1943. Later, long after he
had grown up and become a grand
master, his public appearances were
disappointing; he did not live up to
early expectations for chess bril-
liancy.

Although he played on the first
board in the Spanish national team,
he did not belong to the international elite, and many remembered
the days when the boy Arturo had
earned marvelous, yet premature,

praise. Another whiz kid was Samuel Reshevsky, who began his career in Poland at age four and
crowned it as an adult with several
U.S. championships. At age five, he
first appeared in Vienna, where his
prowess at the same infuriated
chess notables against whom he
played. The Viennese felt compelled
to bring out their strongest weapon
against him, the Yugoslavian Milan
Vidmar. In his memoirs, Vidmar
admits how he had underestimated
the little player. "Very soon, you
see, I felt that my opponent had a

*Louis XVI playing chess against an
officer of the guard. If he should lose
the game, which was always a possibility, he could always use the excuse that he was distracted, by
beautiful women. In fact, more than
one present-day grand master has
been only too happy to use this excuse.*

Below: *There is a first time for everything. The first chess genius was the American Paul Morphy, considered to be the greatest combination player of all time.*

Above: *Thanks are due to the Englishman Howard Staunton for the first chess magazine and the first international tournament in modern times. Staunton was a great player and the illegitimate son of the Duke of Carlisle.*

hand of iron. He began to constrict me; he pushed harder, harder ..." By calling up all his knowledge and ability, the adult master just managed to win, causing the little boy to drop his head on the chessboard and cry fervently. He was, despite his strength over the board, a child. "But what should I have done?" wrote Vidmar with mixed feelings. "Let myself be defeated?"

Even in his sixties, Reshevsky participated in important tournaments and demonstrated a perseverance that marks the other great grand master. Emanuel La-

Siegbert Tarrasch (left), *Richard Réti* (center) *and Aaron Nimzowitsch* (right): *Three exceptional players, three chess authors and three leading theoreticians. Not one of them ever won the World Championship although Tarrasch came very close to it. He loved open positions*

sker was nearly 70 when he won third place in Moscow against 19 players, some of them very strong competitors. Vassily Smyslov, who at 36 had lost his world-champion title, was 62 years old when he played in the qualifications for the world championship in 1984, defeat-

ing a Hungarian young enough to have been his son. Smyslov had demonstrated what Steinitz meant by his statement, shortly before his death, "Although I'm old, I allow no one to put a finger in my mouth, for I will bite."

In 1948, the 83-year-old German grand master Jacques Mieses, whose career lasted 60 years, won against an 84-year-old player in a simultaneous tournament. "Youth has triumphed!" exclaimed Mieses enthusiastically.

This unique game favors unique personalities. Despite ironclad rules

and taught how to construct and use them to advantage. Réti and Nimzowitsch preferred closed positions and showed what was hidden in them. Tarrasch advanced the middle pawn into the center as quickly as possible.

and numerous strategic and tactical requirements the game allows players to show their individuality. Many great players develop a distinct style. For example, Paul Morphy, born in the United States in 1837, is considered the combinational theoreticians' theoretician.

Left: *Both World Championship contests between Alekhine and Bogolyubov were substitutes. If Alexander Alekhine had chosen the strongest player as his opponent he would have allowed his old rival Capablanca to seek his revenge. However, the Russian protected himself by choosing to play against the decidedly weaker Ukrainian player. The picture shows the two experienced players at the Café König in Berlin. Watching them is an even older player, Emanuel Lasker.*

It was "The Golden Age of Chess" and this was the title used by the Yugoslavian grand master Milan Vidmar for his vivid description.
Vidmar also wrote of the prodigy Samuel Reshevsky (far below left), a well-known personality who, though small in stature was a player of immense skill into his old age.
Vasily Smyslov (far below right), who almost became a professional singer instead of a grand master, also stayed young at the chess board for decades.

No one in grand master chess has devised admiration so freely, so unconstrainedly or so directly as Morphy. The admiration of future generations grew with the realization that he had marked well, even if only instinctively, principles of strategy that would not be explained theoretically until decades later. Although Morphy had at an early age defeated the world's elite players, he withdrew from chess to pursue

his career as a lawyer. Another U.S. player, Frank Marshall, born in 1877, was also a brilliant tactician. Marshall's style depended on ingenious, even comic ideas, which enraptured his audiences. Marshall introduced the chess term "swindle"

off by striking sacrifices. Tal's brilliant sacrifice posed problems that his opponents may have solved in three weeks but could not possibly work out in three hours, a tactic which cannot be faulted. It is not surprising, however, that Tal lost

"I think that I play in rather the same way as Jack Dempsey boxes. From the first bell of the first round Dempsey begins hitting his opponent and from then on doesn't give him

a chance to even get his thoughts together." In these words the American Frank Marshall described the style that had made him so popular with the public. He was a giant of a man who loved large ties and thick cigars.

Previous double page: *The Chess Olympics are team World Championships. In the fall of 1982 they were held in Lucerne. Ninety-nine men's teams and 53 teams of women took part. The men played in teams of four, the women with three per team and, in addition, there were reserve players, two for the men's and one for the women's teams.*

to describe faulty combinations, that are intended to confuse the opponent and cost him time. Mikail Tal, born in Riga in 1936, can be considered the greatest swindler. He was a grand master, a world champion, and a wizard. His combinations were like fireworks set

the world championship title after a year to his predecessor, the deliberate and methodical Michail Botvinnik. That is the Achilles' heel of great tacticians: successes that are based on wonderful combinations are impressive but usually not very lasting. Tal himself remarked ironically, "There are two types of sacrifices: correct ones and mine."

Tal's diametric opposite was Tigran Petrosyan, an Armenian born in 1929. With unshakable equanimity, he placed pawns and pieces in the most favorable posi-

tions and did not insist on complications. Petrosyan had a steady style of play, difficult to outwit. Once, however, in a decisive hour, he was unfaithful to his character: Petrosyan badly wanted to stop Bobby Fischer's triumphant advance in Buenos Aires in 1971, so during the first game of the competition, Pet-

rosyan surprised his opponent and hundreds of knowledgeable observers with a prepared, yet risky, variation. Fischer got caught in a terrible attack and, although he defended himself artfully, the audience expected a spectacular defeat. However, Petrosyan would pay for pursuing a train of thought he was not able to set forth consistently. His attack petered out, and his opponent took the initiative, event-

ually winning the game. It was as if the great Petrosyan were being punished for his bold attempt to imitate a different style of play.

Robert (Bobby) Fischer, born in the United States in 1943, was one of the greatest natural talents. Never satisfied at being a good player, he was filled with an unbridled desire to be the best at chess. It was this mixture of talent and determination, that made him

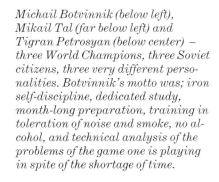

Michail Botvinnik (below left), Mikail Tal (far below left) and Tigran Petrosyan (below center) – three World Champions, three Soviet citizens, three very different personalities. Botvinnik's motto was; iron self-discipline, dedicated study, month-long preparation, training in toleration of noise and smoke, no alcohol, and technical analysis of the problems of the game one is playing in spite of the shortage of time.

Tal, on the other hand, relied on spontaneous, bewildering, complicated ideas. If his opponent was confused, the game was already half

won. Tal was thought of as a magician, Petrosyan as a temporizer. He placed his chessmen on the best possible squares and then waited to see how his opponent would react — just to prove that it had been a bad idea.

Wolfgang Unzicker (above left) played against all of them. Here he is at the Chess Olympics in Leipzig in 1960 before a game against 17-year-old Bobby Fischer (above right).

"The most remarkable thing about Bobby Fischer is the maturity of his game, a maturity that was already apparent at an incredibly early age. Of course he can play brilliant combinations, but from the beginning he has displayed a total understanding of strategy that is truly amazing." Thus wrote Reuben Fine about Robert James Fischer, known as Bobby. The general public mostly thought of him as an eccentric, which was partly true. His demands for regular payment and complete quiet were unusual at the time and therefore seemed eccentric, even though these later became a matter of course and benefited all his colleagues.

so overpowering. Never had a player before him succeeded at becoming a grand master at age 15, nor had a young man, to whom everything seemed to come easily, ever acquired such an encyclopedic knowledge of chess. Fischer liked to combine a modest immediate objective with a slight improvement in position. Since he made combinations incessantly, his position became more favorable from move to move. This specialty made his best games continually exciting and also gave the false impression that Fischer was an offensive player. Fischer was, in fact, the most dynamic, adventurous positional player of the century. He did not merely want to win but to crush his opponent. Therefore, he simply stopped competing after winning all of the matches necessary to become world champion. He took no offense at the accusation that he had a killer instinct. The killer instinct was a gift that the Soviet grand master Paul Keres, born in 1916, lacked, according to friends, who tried to explain the reason he never ascended to the chess throne, although Keres had followers throughout the world. He was as excellent a combinational as a positional player, as perfect a strategist as a tactician. In writing about "individual style," Euwe quoted the widespread opinion that Keres had the "ideal style." The answer to the question of which player was most deserving of the world championship but never won it is Keres. In addition to his chess talent, he had an elegant personal style and winning manners. Since

individuality has such an enduring effect, can opponents also take advantage of it? This is an important question in competition. Emanuel Lasker, who was born in 1868 in Brandenburg of Jewish descent, was considered to be a master of psychological analysis. Lasker, who was world champion for 27 years, won many matches that to all appearances he should have lost. Some even accused him of using black magic. In truth, he only wanted to lead his opponent into a false sense of security so that the opponent would become careless. He changed

his style constantly to confuse his opponent. Lasker, unlike Tarrasch, did not believe in beauty, but only in effectiveness and practicality. He thought that the quality of a move depended on the opponent. Of course, Lasker knew that practical psychology could not replace expertise in chess, but it could augment expertise. Alexander Alekhine, among many others, tried to

Left: *Garry Kasparov is not only an experienced player but also a formidably quick thinker. Simultaneous performances like the one held in Zurich in September 1986 hardly seem to bother him at all. At the end of a performance he seems as full of energy as at the beginning.*

Below left: *Max Euwe in contest with Michail Botvinnik.*

Below center: *Alexander Alekhine, the son of a Czarist officer, was an emigrant. In 1921 he went to Paris, became a French citizen and obtained a doctorate in law at the Sorbonne. Euwe and Alekhine were opponents in the 1935 and 1937 World Championships.*

profit from Lasker's wisdom. In his book about the New York Tournament of 1927, he expressed his annoyance at a harmless opening move by Marshall. "That the move," he wrote, "is a technical error is open to question, but it is certainly a psychological one. There simply is something that the older masters [excepting Dr. Lasker] must grant our generation of chess players: not

cunning, which too often is a sign of weakness of character, but the conviction, won through experience, that above all a knowledge of human nature and a penetration of the opponent's psychology is necessary for chess, for the battle of chess. Formerly, one played only with

Above left: *Although he brought fame to the Soviet Union, the Estonian Paul Keres never felt especially happy there.*

Above right: *José Capablanca, a cosmopolitan citizen from Cuba, was on the best of terms with the Cuban government. He had been taken, pro forma, into the diplomatic service.*

The grand master Akiba Rubinstein (1882 – 1961) was one of the strongest players in the world from 1907 to 1914. He was considered to be a superb tactician and he developed opening strategy.

pieces — but we play (or endeavor to, at least) with the opponent, the enemy, with his will, his nerves, his special likes, idiosyncracies, and — last but not least — with his vanity."

Alekhine hated nothing more than passivity. He endeavored to seize the initiative and was unequaled in the art of breathing life into boring positions. Above all, he loved complications. He also had his concept of beauty, although discovering it only in entanglement, in the diversity of an ideal. It is ironic that his greatest adversary, José Raúl Capablanca, was a genius of simplicity. Alekhine, born in 1892, defeated Capablanca, four years his elder, in a tough competition that lasted 34 games. From that point on he avoided all return matches, a practice permissible at the time. For Capablanca, who had started as a child prodigy and completed his tournaments as a grand seigneur, true strategy and tactics were self-evident. Simplicity was not foolishness to him, but rather, it was proof that he had gotten to the bottom of things. The world of chess has produced only five definite geniuses to date: Morphy, Lasker, Capablanca, Alekhine and Fischer. It is uncertain whether anyone will be added to this list in our day. Anatoli Karpov, born in 1951, has often been compared with Capablanca; younger by 12 years, Gary Kasparov has been compared with Alekhine. It is strange that the contrariness of two natures should be repeated. Karpov's ideal is absolute infallibility, which leads to a very circumspect, yet rather dry game.

Kasparov fancies boldness and imagination. He has unleashed many a storm and survived.

The blind also play. What their eyes cannot see, their fingers can feel. Each blind contestant has a portable chess set in which each piece has a peg underneath and each square a hole. Black and white

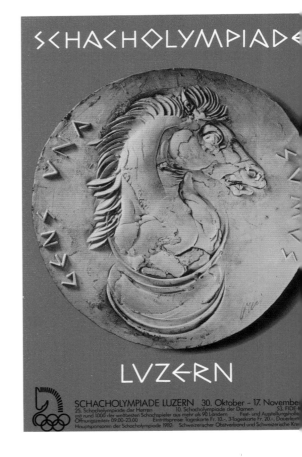

27TH CHESS OLYMPIAD - DUBAI '86

pieces are differentiated by means of detail that can be felt; black and white squares by their relative heights. Blind players announce the moves they wish to make orally. The blind are generous and permit players who still have some limited sense of sight to participate in their international tournaments. Another variation of blind chess consists of voluntarily playing without the board. A player with much experience, a good memory, and a precise imagination sits behind a screen, communicates with his opponent verbally and sees the many positions of the game only in his mind's eye. Some ambitious contestants manage a couple of dozen games simultaneously, exercising an intellectual sport, the danger of which has often been emphasized.

A third type of blindness is a deficiency of the player. At times, it even befalls the most capable masters. Anyone who is immune to this blindness has had to work hard. For what does "seeing" mean? Does it mean perceiving, noticing, determining, recognizing or seeing through something? Actually, the player sees everything. Each piece is there and it is clear which squares the pieces may occupy. The player stares at the board continually, yet too often the scales fall from his eyes only after his opponent's answer.

"Seeing" is a technical term in chess and denotes the correct intellectual processing of a perception. Some do not "see" that their combination of eight moves has a "hole" after the fifth; others do not even notice that their pawns stand "en prise," *i.e.,* endangered and uncovered. A nearly unbelievable case of chess blindness occurred at a qualifying tournament for the world championship. Robert Hübner, born in Germany in 1948, usually sees an extraordinary amount: combinations, developments, dangers, in short, everything in the offing. This

Since 1927, chess Olympics, Team World Championships have been organized by FIDE. Four players per country participate. These events are held every two years. The emblems of the Chess Olympics held in Malta (1908), Lucerne (1982), Thessaloniki (1984), Dubai (1986) and Thessaloniki (1988). The artist Hans Erni designed the commemorative medal for the event in Lucerne in 1982.

Robert Hübner, a classical scholar and papyrologist, is not always a very lucky but always a very conscientious player. He likes jotting down in his written commentaries the meanderings of his mind. The possible variations with which he fills out his analyses are usually five times longer than the games themselves.

Two opponents forming a unit. The bronze statue "Chess Players" from the year 1940 by Gerhard Marcks certainly gives us this impression. A semicircle is formed by the crowns of two heads and the two backs arching over the board of a shared game. The loser will participate in the victory, for without the loser's inspiration, the stronger player will not be the victor.

time, however — he was White — a conclusive four or five move mate escaped him. In the fair hall of the Swiss "City of Clocks," Biel, hundreds of onlookers "saw" how Hübner could defeat Petrosyan fairly easily. The excitement in the hall was based on the general astonishment at White's reluctance to make a move and Black's reluctance to capitulate. Hübner, who was seated, rubbed his head with his hands, while Petrosyan, who was standing, had laid his folded hands on his stomach, as if nothing was amiss. Hübner was in no hurry, but Petrosyan was. Yet Hübner did not take a path, clear as daylight, to victory; instead he became muddled, and in the end lost the game.

Savielly Tartakover wrote the wittiest book about mistakes. It consists of self-made aphorisms or, as his readers soon called them, "Tartakoverisms," that are captivating for their paradoxicality. At first glance, it appears as if Tartakower's sayings about chess mistakes were errors in reasoning. However, they are intended to provoke contradiction, and in the end, the lead to the realization that the intellectual skirmish between the author and the reader would have ended in a draw, at least. Here are some examples.

Left: *The king lifts himself up and grows until he is larger than life and then slips into the role of the player. On the board he is the piece around which everything revolves, the piece on which the opponent's thoughts of capture focus. Is the over-dimensional size given to him by Max Ernst not a reflection of his importance? The idea, of course, that comes to mind from the title of his bronze statue from the year 1944, "The King plays with his Queen," is just fun and games, a game of thoughts with a pensive game. Just as the little Queen put horns on her great King.*

"The king is the weakest piece!" proclaimed Morphy, then attacked the king and won. "The pawn is the weakest piece," proclaimed Steinitz, attacked it and won. "Everything is weak, everything can be weakened!" youth proclaims, attacks everything and wins. This is how Savielly Tartakover (above) wrote about chess. Everything, even the reader, can be weakened. Why should he learn the rules of chess when Tartakover also said, "Chess rules are only there to be replaced?"

"Some part of a mistake is always correct," to which can be added: for that reason precisely, mistakes are so tempting. Sometimes a player neglects to make other important considerations. Often, he will think only of the effect, and not of the side effects that may defeat his purpose.

"Mistakes are there to be made." The eradication of mistakes from tournaments would spell their end. A flawless game is boring and ends in a draw. Brilliant games re-

In 1937 and 1938, *Paul Klee* was repeatedly interested by the rhythmic structure of the chessboard. Like Arnold Schönberg in his twelve-tone system, he recognized certain regularities: "Each tone is set via its relationship to the preordained base line, astronomical laws are in force although they are uncontrollable individually. Reasoning and enchantment come together and become one in what is called 'wisdom, initiation, in a belief in the stars, the figures'."

quire mistakes that are microscopically small or even (in the sense that some part of a mistake is always correct) highly intelligent. Furthermore, mistakes have to be made for educational purposes. Without defeat, there is no thirst for knowledge; without the latter, no success. In addition, whoever wants to induce his opponent to make mistakes must have learned about them beforehand. The most expedient way of doing so is to make them oneself. This brings to mind the simple saying, "One learns only through mistakes." In fact, Tartakover did say this. However, he erred in one thing: "only" is an inadmissible exaggeration.

"A positivist view of the game: usually, sacrifices merely serve to prove that mistakes have preceded them." In the language of chess, "sacrifice" is a word full of promises. The gong is struck resoundingly, the grand combination must follow. However, a sacrificial move is quite an unusual measure, due to its drama, and gives rise to the suspicion that the player's usual means have failed. Often, a sacrifice seems to be an act of desperation although a noteworthy one.

"The second-best move is often the only correct one." The opponent, after all, must be thought capable of secretly preparing mentally for the very best move. There is a certain probability that he is providing for the second-best move to a much lesser; there is even the pleasing possibility that he considers the second-best move to be so weak that

he will counter it with a random and, therefore, wrong answer.

"In chess, there is only one mistake: overestimating one's opponent. Everything else is either bad luck or weakness." Educators prefer to warn against underestimation. It is evident that underestimation may lead to holding back in competition — just as overestimation may. But what is to be done if an adversary's superiority is beyond all doubt? In that case (this is no longer Tartakover speaking). The player might try depersonalizing his opponent by taking only in squares and pieces.

Stefan Zweig wrote his chess novella "The Royal Game" during the Nazi era. In this story, chess is not an amusing, secondary subject but the main pastime of the chief characters. The drama is initially rooted in the persecution of the hero by the National Socialists; later, however, the focus is on the peculiarities of the game and two players. The plot is woven so expertly and the style is so brilliant that one would have to forgive the author had he used some unclear terminology. Yet Zweig did not slip up. He knew his way around the board so that his excellent psychological portrayals never contradict the content. The powerful yet narrow-minded international master, the imaginary Mirko Czentović, is captured just as well as his inspired and sensitive opponent. The novella's readers may consider it improbable that one learns to play without chess pieces by mentally playing against oneself, yet the author's empathy is proved in these

63

Sketch by Hans Fronius from the first edition of the "Schachnovelle" by Stefan Zweig, published by Bermann-Fischer in 1943 when exiled in Sweden.

Right page, above: *The World Champion is an unappealing expert. The true hero of the novel and of the film is an unknown Dr. B., who is more sensitive and maybe even more talented than the title holder. In spite of this, he is not able to defeat him. In the film version of the "Schachnovelle" by Stefan Zweig, Mario Adorf played the World Champion, Czentovic, and Curd Jürgens his challenger.*

Right: *These are the pawns and pieces held by a master. Although they were designed by Nathaniel Cook they have been named after Howard Staunton. The pieces are highly stylized. One can see that the knight is a horse's head and that the rook resembles a tower, but the pawn does not look like a man of the land, nor does the queen appear to have female traits.*

very passages. Despite this, he erred in one point. Studying a collection of tournaments consisting of only 150 games does not enable even the most brilliant mind to compete with the world champion, even if that study is as thorough, intense, and exhaustive as Stefan Zweig portrays it. There is too little illustrative material. Also, knowledge of chess alone is not sufficient; that knowledge must be deepened and refined by practice, which is precisely what the hero of this exciting work does not have during his imprisonment.

Vladimir Nabokov avoided a similar error when writing his novel about the life of an excellent player in, *Lushin's Defense*. The fictional character, Lushin, as a child scarcely understood the rules of chess before he started to replay games published in newspapers and to understand everything that happens in the games. Finally, he needs to glance only once at the chessboard and pieces when reading the notations. However, this does not comprise all of Lushin's chess training. Certainly, Nabokov, a good author, rated the power of the printed word remarkably highly, as did Zweig. And certainly, many beginners devour the technical literature. Nevertheless, the chess player receives his primary training in competition. He will try his strength against many opponents, and thus increase it.

Each match has two fathers. Only victories in which difficulties have to be overcome are inspiring. The loser's claim to fame is the creation of these difficulties. Many players who have been defeated in competition have accomplished more than some winners. In order

for a mental work of art to arise, the opponents must have enough time — four or five hours for 40 moves is a good compromise between the requirements of the game and the stamina of the players. At present, "active chess" is spreading. The audience's impatience is taken into account by limiting the time available for reflection to 30 minutes on each player's clock. Yet the fastest thoughts are rarely the most profound. And it is the later, which cannot be produced offhand, that have given chess its standing as an admirable exercise of the intellect.

Following double page:
Nissam Engel painted this oil "Chess Composition" in the style of a collage made up of many individual boards and chess pieces.

The oil painting "Überschach" from 1937 is the work of Paul Klee. He varied the pattern of the chess-board, enlarging the white squares in proportion to the black which he also changed. Klee brought life to a well-known pattern. The chess player, lost in deep thought, often has similar experiences. The squares c4, e6, h3 can each represent either a threat or a promise and so they become larger than life.

Nissan Engel

"Via the squares on a chessboard, the Indians explain the movement of time and the age, the higher influences which control the world and the ties which link chess with the human soul."

The Arabian historian Al-Masudi in 947

THE KING AND HIS TRAIN

Miniature and text from the handwritten manuscript (1407) by Jacobo da Cessole. Bavarian State Library, Munich.
"The king should resemble as nearly as possible a living king. He should be seated in a palace and wear purple robes to show that he is graced with virtues and mercy."

Opposite:
Left: *Arabian king, modeled in the Indian style, ivory, 8th – 9th century.*

Right: *An 18th century Turkish king, ivory inlaid.*

The American psychologist Reuben Fine was a respected chess player as well as a psychoanalyst. He wrote an odd book, *The Psychology of the Chess Player,* in which he claimed that the king is a father figure, although a weakened one. Fine claimed that those who particularly like this chess piece are those who consider themselves to be very important and indispensable. In addition, Fine viewed the king as a phallic symbol.

THE KING

Not all chess players are especially literate and may not be familiar with Fine's book, but whoever reads it has to acknowledge the impact of the author's comparisons regarding the royal chess piece and the possible analogies to the grand masters of chess. Even amateurs recognize how things stand with the king. He is impressive, and in need of help. His value is diametrically opposed to his strength. Whereas other pieces can cross the board in one move, the king creeps from one square to another at a snail's pace. At the start of a game, he is completely useless, yet must be guarded like Fort Knox.

Even centuries ago, careful players were anxious to get this splendid, idle piece out of harm's way as early as possible. Traditionally, the king stands in the middle of the edge of the board. He is even too slow to flee into the corner. Thus,

An abstract Arabian bone figure of the 8th – 9th century.

Arabian-Egyptian, rock crystal, late 9th – early 11th century.

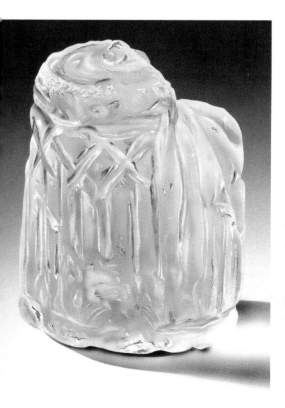

once during a game, but only under certain circumstances, he is allowed to jump sideways two squares on his rank, exchanging sides with the rook. This move, "castling," was not introduced until the 16th century. This move may be considered a systemic outrage, because not only are two moves combined into one, but two major pieces are permitted to sneak past each other on one and the same rank. By the way, only amateurs and devotees do not care which piece is moved first, the king or the rook. It would be more logical to proceed with both hands, strictly synchronically, as in piano playing. However, since only a few chess fans can play piano as well as grand master Mark Taimanov, another type of logic was developed: All moves, including castling, must be clear and indisputable. Moreover, according to the rule for "touch — move," the player has committed himself to his move the instant the tips of his thumb and index finger touch the piece in question. If he were allowed to touch the rook first in castling, he would not be committing himself because that would admit the possibility of his only wanting to move the rook, if only for a short moment. If, on the other hand, he first moves his king two squares to the left or right, it is immediately obvious to his opponent and the audience that he is castling on the king's or queen's side.

The king may stay put until the 30th or 40th move, yet after the lines of battle have thinned, he bursts forth suddenly. The passive, endangered piece becomes active

and extremely dangerous. The recognition of this transition requires a sharp chess mind, and the final battle begins. No other piece reveals such a change in temperament, not even the pawn, for when it is queened, it is no longer a pawn. Whereas it would have been idiocy to let the most important piece limp to the middle of the board in mid-game, the motto of the endgame is "centralize the king!" Although up to this point the king was concerned only with his own defence and often was not capable of providing it alone, he now becomes involved and takes the offensive. It is a pity that chess theorists — let alone the practicians — so rarely turn to philosophy for intellectual support. Otherwise, the opposition of potency and action would have found its way into chess literature. The first is, in a completely unerotic sense, innate ability, the latter its application. Not until the endgame does the king show his power; for example, his ability to keep his own and eight other squares under his thumb. His qualities as a pawn-stopper and a pawn-catcher clearly manifest themselves then, too. He can even overpower the mighty rooks on the diagonal. His measured pace is no longer reminiscent of hobbling on crutches but, rather, of the composure and self-confidence of true majesty. At this point, chess becomes the royal game in fact.

Of course, chess can be royal in the sense of its being a matter of life or death for the king in mid-game. After all, the goal of a game is mate, occurring when the king cannot be

Above, left and right:
Germany or Austria, figure in wood, 20th century.

An Italian ceramic piece of the first half of the 20th century.

Left: *Scandinavian, walrus tusk, ca. 1200.*

Below, left and right:
Israel, soapstone, 20th century.

Portugal, porcelain, 20th century.

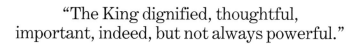

"The King dignified, thoughtful, important, indeed, but not always powerful."

Christian Morgenstern

saved from an immediate threat. However, this rarely occurs in tournament halls, because chess masters prefer to yield to an inevitable fate before the final blow. Whoever has not been able to stave off the knockout at least wants to be clever enough to see it coming. At the same time, it is a matter of tacit agreement that the honorable adversary is above the crass mistakes that could ruin a winning position at the last minute. A loser who cannot bring himself to shake hands with his opponent and congratulate him when capitulating lays his king on its side. Knocking it over accidentally — sleeves get caught on the pieces easily — is considered a bad omen by superstitious people.

Often, another fate befalls the kings in tournaments; after the players have deigned to touch them only once, when castling, a ministering spirit, who also brings the other 30 pieces back home, places the king in the middle of the board as a symbol of unity. This denotes a draw — a word with a bad reputation among chess lovers. It is not that they are upset when they are denied a victory; on the contrary, they accept the sharing of points as middle Europeans do a cloudy day. Grand masters are great ones for draws. If the position is balanced and cannot be shaken by White or Black except at great risk, the contest is a standoff. Sometimes, the battle actually has raged and consumed the energy of both players, so that it is only right and proper that neither of them be branded a loser. Not every eminent

a success, namely for the weaker player and for Black. Also tournament participants who want an easy Thursday because they had to slave away on Wednesday and will face a merciless opponent on Friday may indeed expect general sympathy for a draw. Another reason may be a player's reflection that if he can no longer win fourth place, why should he endanger fifth through overzealousness. It may also be the case, although it will be denied, that draws are agreed beforehand, *i.e.,* that the games are "fixed." This tacit agreement does not require much conversation. Certain moves, even during the opening, have to be interpreted as signals. If they are answered by the corresponding moves, the rest of the game is only a matter of preserving the illusion of fighting for

authority has Alexander Alekhine's gift of getting so much out of an apparently "dead" position that suddenly a path to victory appears.

Many reasons for a draw are often given. They start with the rationalization that a draw is actually

Above: *Indian, early 19th century.*

Above left and right:
Indonesia, fruitwood, 20th century.

China, ivory, late 19th or early 20th century.

Denmark, ceramic, 20th century.
Right: *India, ivory, 20th century.*

Below, from left to right:
Alpine Germany, painted wood, late 18th century.

India, wood topped with ivory, 19th century.

France, ivory, late 18th – early 19th century.

Germany, Meissen porcelain, designed 1752/53.

Scandinavian, walrus bone, 12 – 13th century.

victory. Sometimes, contestants even dispense with that and end their play after 10 or 12 moves. The chess world disdains such "grand master" or "parlor" draws.

Peace pacts that have made chess history include the draws of the Soviet grand masters who considered it their duty to keep down the only foreigner they thought capable of becoming world champion. They spared their intellectual powers with each other to keep them fresh for the games against the U.S. "class enemy," Robert Fischer. He complained bitterly about this treatment. When he attained his goal in 1972, many agreed with him that he had wrested the highest title not only from Boris Spassky, but from the entire Soviet chess nation. Petar

Trifunović, the deceased Yugoslavian grand master, once told how he had been charged by func-

tionaries to win a game against Fischer at all costs. That was easier said than done, especially because Fischer, who was difficult to defeat even when he was Black, was playing White in this game. Trifunović argued that it would be audacious enough to pledge a draw in view of such an opponent — but a victory? Words were to no avail, the man from Dalmatia must make the impossible come to pass. In his desperation he unearthed a rarely played Ruy Lopez defence, in which it was considered disadvantageous for Black to be conciliatory, but only because the theorists of opening moves had overseen an improvement that Trifunović discovered. However, as the game began, Fischer became suspicious. He was astonished that such an extremely sound player would choose so doubtful a defence, and was thus doubly alert. If Fischer had followed the advice that all authors give to White, he might have stumbled. Instead, he won: "For he did not, play by the book. He played correctly!"

The less professional the player, the smaller the desire for a draw. It does not easily cross the mind of an amateur sitting comfortably in his living room to offer his friend a draw merely because their positions are equal and have no prospects. Secretly, he feels that a new perspective will open up as quickly and reliably as the next mistake. The chess lover is characterized by the player in the following anecdote: One player had just refused the offer of a draw, something which astonished his adversary. "Are you

playing to win?" "No." "What? Are you playing to lose?" "Of course not." "Well then, what is it you want?" "To play!" In contrast to most professionals, who would terminate the game, this type of player remains undaunted even if he is one piece down. He would like to wait and see his king in trouble.

If it's a case of do or die — that is, a case of the king's doing or dying — two types of undecided finishes tend to be dramatic, stalemate and perpetual check. Stalemate involves making a virtue of necessity and making the presumed loser the hero of the day. The stalemated player is the player whose turn it is and who must move some piece but cannot make a legal move. This predicament is charged to the other side. An unthreatened king that

Below, from left to right:
India (?), ivory painted yellow-red, 19th century.
Italy, ivory, from "Aristocrats," late 18th century.
Venice, hollow glass, 18th century.

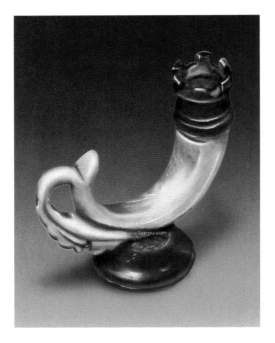

King, Jewish, ivory, 18th century.

King, Germany, Bauhaus, pearwood, designed by Josef Hartwig, 1923/24.

cannot move is by no means mated. If it were, no game could ever start because the king is wedged in even before the first move. On the other hand, perpetual check denotes innocuous chess — if it were dangerous, it would not last forever. It is a brilliant case of repeated moves, meaning a maneuver that recurs three times in a row.

Perhaps some day there will be only three kings left in the world: the White, the Black, and the English. Chess is in the best of health and has outlived the monarchic orders whose spirit it so unabashedly reflects. Much has changed over the past few centuries, even with respect to decency, the sense of justice, and war and traffic but not chess. Even republicans, who have no love for flesh-and-blood kings, play chess passionately. Proponents of a classless society think nothing of the fact that the two rooks are stronger than the two bishops, and they in turn stronger than two pawns. Atheists protect their Staunton kings even though they bear crosses on their heads.

Vive le roi!

The queen is a dashing lady. At first, she patiently waits next to the king but soon goes her own way. She is the piece that can and may do almost anything. She steps to the side like a king, moves forward like a pawn, runs like a bishop, and charges like a rook. She is forbidden to move only

THE QUEEN

as strangely as a knight. She is in the enemy camp in the twinkling of an eye. In one move, she wheels around from the queen's to the king's wing. By a mere small movement she influences the entire constellation of forces. By way of illustration is Alekhine's victory during the world championship match against Capablanca in Buenos Aires 1927. In the 34th round Alekhine moved his white queen only one square to the left, yet this negligible change from e2 to d2 elicited the following enthusiastic commentary: "The versatility of this move delights me. I think it earns the mark 'beautiful', as it encompasses the board in the full sense of the word."

The queen is able to fascinate with her great strength. It was this verve for which the unknown reformers of the late Middle Ages must have longed as they proceeded to

Above: *Queen, India, wood topped with ivory, 19th century.*

Left: *Danish, bone (walrus), 13th century.*

Below, from left to right:

India (?), ivory, 19th century (2 pieces).

Ecuador, painted Tagua wood, 20th century.

France, ivory polychrome, late 18th – early 19th century (precursor of the so-called Napoleon pieces).

give the queen a much larger radius of action than the king. At that time, the queen took the place of the vizier, the Arabic minister, a weak figure who was only allowed to take the smallest possible steps on the diagonal.

This sex change has long engrossed chess historians. They are still groping for an explanation, and some strange theories have been developed. Actually, chess could have remained purely a man's world, as the female figure does the same things as the other combatants, although more vehemently: move and attack. However, the powerful are not just keen on power, but also on love. It was logical to grant the king a queen; as the *rex* has his *regina* in old Latin chess texts, so too in modern German does the *König* have his *Dame* and the *roi* his *reine* in French.

Some historians credit the *Minnesang,* a medieval literary genre full of passionate, although spiritual, veneration of women, with influencing the game of chess. It is conceivable that the exaltation with which the "Noble Lady" was beheld, adored and idolized rubbed off on the rules of the game, although if that was the case it's strange that the queen was not also allowed to jump. Dr. Jacob Silbermann, trainer of the Romanian national chess team from 1949 to 1963, had a different theory. He thought that Joan d'Arc, the maid of Orleans, was the

whore. In the 15th century, she was burned at the stake as a heretic, and no one knew at that time that she would be declared a saint in the 20th century. In a story by Werner Bergengruen, who describes a chess game in highly dramatic circumstances, a Christian slave tells his Arabian partner, who has just given "check the vizier," "We also say Virgin after the Mother of God." Similarly, Professor Joachim Petzold, a chess historian from Dresden, recent interpreted the transformation of the dilapidated minister to a full-blooded, lively queen as a product of the adoration of the Virgin Mary. He noted the sentiment of the builders of the Parisian cathedral, Notre Dame, a

model for the chess queen. The French heroine was a young woman who was braver than the men around her and led an entire army.

However, it must be borne in mind that Joan of Arc was not liked at all times and in all places. Shakespeare portrayed her as a witch and

Left: *Southern Italy, ivory, first half of the 12th century.*

Below, from left to right:

Germany, Meissen porcelain, 18th century.

Israel (from the "King Solomon Game") soapstone (steatite), polychrome, 20th century.

Italy, "Aristocrats," ivory game, late 18th century.

French (from "Napoleon and Marie Louise"), early 19th century.

Italian, African-ivory figure, late 18th century.

France, ivory, polychrome, late 18th – early 19th century.

sentiment that he thought chess fans also shared in those times. There is just one thing that does not fit. In a thousand sculptures and countless paintings, we see the Mother of God sitting, enthroned, sometimes kneeling or standing, usually radiating tranquility, yet never in a hurry. The queen of the 64 squares is a complete contrast. If necessary, she races like a Fury, back and forth. Finally, mention should be made of a piece of information from 1616 because it is so chivalrous. In Gustavus Selenus' 1616 chess handbook of extraordinary intellectual tenability, the question is posed of why precisely the womenfolk have been assigned the most encompassing tasks. After the author has mentally brushed aside the usual remark about Amazons, he surmises that the anonymous inventor of the queen's moves "wanted to intimate that women ignite, as it were, the hearts

> "The best move in chess,
> as in life,
> is always – the one that is made."
>
> *Savielly Tartakover*

and spirits of soldiers in battle and combat." This is at least a charming fib, although it tends to make the lady here called a queen look like a slut. Therefore, the author hurried to add that the queen advises her husband wisely and judiciously in important affairs. Gustavus Selenus must have known: behind this pseudonym hid the sage Duke August II of Braunschweig-Lüneburg.

The queen is better suited for the double attack than other pieces, who actually are also capable of it. This is the essence of tactics. Whoever considers risking a bishop or knights should think hard before even moving his queen. Safety-first specialists warn against advancing the queen in the opening. Variations in which she is the first to take a pawn may be correct, yet such a move is rarely advisable. Choosing squares b2 and b7 is considered a temptation to which a player should yield only after the most careful reflection. The possibility of a trap must always be borne in mind. A trap is a particularly treacherous way of seizing a piece. It is encircled, something almost demeaning to the player of a queen. The queen, who was created to run off in eight directions, suddenly does not know which way to turn, because all possible squares are either occupied or endangered. Rooks, bishops, and knights can also be ensnared and then captured, yet the fall of a queen causes the most annoyance because it creates the most glee on the other side.

Germany, porcelain manufactured by Frankenthal, modeled by K. Linck, 1765/70.

Left page, above: *Danish, bone (walrus), 13th century.*

Right: *China, red-stained ivory, late 19th, early 20th century.*

Below, from left to right:

Chinese, a queen rocking her baby (the Infante), 17th century.

Russia, "Boyar", wood with colored decoration, 20th century.

Italy, ceramic, first half of the 20th century.

Germany or Austria, wood, 20th century.

Scandinavian, bone (walrus), circa 1200.

Ever since tournaments have been played, the sacrifice of a queen has been regarded by onlookers as the ultimate pleasure. When a player voluntarily relinquishes his best piece, he raises the question of whether or not self-mutilation can be restorative. Every sacrifice cries out for compensation, or at least material equalization, if it is not revealed to be simply an enormous mistake. The value of a queen may equal two rooks or three minor pieces, but the decisive "market value" depends on the situation. A sacrifice that inspires enthusiasm has to be more than a somewhat awkward exchange of material; it must aim at the destruction of the adversary's position or the initiation of a checkmating drive. The crazier a sacrifice seems at first glance, the more staggering the realization that

rifice considered impossible by the oldest of old hands.

A queen exchange is remarkable if one queen is well developed and the other, underdeveloped or if one is active and the other passive, or if one spreads terror and the other could not hurt a fly. Frequently a vehement attack falls flat because an idle queen has thrown herself in the path of a high-spirited one. It is the triumph of the principle of equality over the principle of achievement and not everybody likes it.

less makes for more. Bobby Fischer provided the first proof of his great genius when he was 13, in a game whose key move was a queen sac-

Above: Denmark, ceramic, 20th century.

Above left: French (?), ivory, first half of the 16th century.

Below, from left to right:
Chinese, gold filigree, 18th century.
France, ivory, first half of the 19th century.
France, hardwood, early 19th century.
Chinese, ivory, late 17th century.
Java, bamboo, 19th century.

Arabian-Egyptian, rock crystal, late 9th – early 11th century.

Scandinavian, turned bone, late 12th – early 13th century.

Opposite: *Germany (Lower Rhine), bone, second half of the 11th century.*

We have already told the romantic tale about the Arabian princess Dilaram. The charming lady convinces her poorly playing husband to sacrifice his two rooks in order to save her. This story has been handed down and believed for a thousand years. This story proves that rooks have been able to slide across the whole board since ancient Arabian times. At the beginning of a game, however, a rook is nothing but a loi-

THE ROOK

terer, plenty of potency but no action. When a stronger player gives up his rook to a player who is several grades weaker, his generosity is limited. The better player asumes that he will have overpowered his opponent anyway by the time this handicap is noticed.

When the other noblemen have decamped and the king is in safety, thanks to castling, the rooks like to join ranks with each other. Allied rooks are a tactical and strategic trump. They cover each other and protect the king, who scarcely needs to fear a flank attack as long as both guards are doing duty on the susceptible first rank. Whether they do so as peels, church towers, elephants with or without throne-like seats, as chariots or ships with complicated riggings, their appearance

always commands respect. The English still use the Arabic *"rukh"* in calling their castle the rook, and many Continental Europeans use Arabic indirectly when speaking of the "rochade" (castling). Consequently a hard "ch" (as in the Scottish *"loch,"*) is at least as correct as a soft "sh" when pronouncing the word.

The retiring, self-effacing rook is like a pillar of society, lending support to the development of the chessmen during the opening. It also loves to unmask. At the masked balls of earlier times, the masks were lowered at a certain hour, for example, at midnight, absolutely flabbergasting many of the dancers. The philanderer's embarrassment of flirting with the wrong person is similar to a chess player's embarrassment of not noticing the man in the background. For example, a pawn strikes, which the opponent was expecting; behind the pawn is a bishop who then starts moving, which the opponent may also have been expecting; however, behind the bishop, the rook looms as a threat that the opponent has not thought to avoid.

One player who liked to bring the rooks into a position was Aaron Nimzowitsch, born in Riga in 1886. Critics considered some of his maneuvers so bizarre that they coined the term "mysterious rook move." Since Nimzowitsch was vain enough to enjoy this lack of general understanding, he adopted the derogatory word "mysterious" in his own writings. The type of unmasking he had in mind was not meant to introduce

> "To avoid losing a piece,
> many a person has lost the game."
>
> *Savielly Tartakover*

Below, from left to right:

North America, ceramic, 20th century.

Ecuador, Tagua nutwood, 20th century.

Israel, soapstone (steatite), polychrome, 20th century.

Czechoslovakia, porcelain, 20th century.

his own attack so much as to prevent the adversary's rush. Nimzowitsch, a tremendous theorist and an excellent practitioner, thought that one of the main occupations of a really good player was to take preventive measures. Around 1920, not everyone was prepared to believe him. But today, "prophylaxis" is more than just a technical term borrowed from the field of medicine; it is a key concept in modern, high-performance chess.

Often, the secret lies in looking far ahead towards prevention — of dangers, loss of pieces and strategic disadvantages. A witty chess fan once declared that the beauty of a great game was based only on the comments. There are several grains of truth in this exaggeration: the average player may not perceive the

value of a mysterious rook move unless it is explained in the analysis.

Nimzowitsch preached the strength of passivity, yet still did not eliminate activity. The rook brothers guarding the first rank so well, unfold their power when it falls on a half-open or open line. "Rook doubling," a classic tactical device, arouses alarm in the opposition. The danger increases when a player's white rook occupies the seventh and his black rook the second rank and they stay put. It might be thought that a bishop in no less powerful on the diagonals than a rook on the ranks and files. To see the error, it suffices to count: a rook, no matter where it stands, can aim at up to 14 squares, whereas a bishop has to be in the middle of the board to reach a maximum of 13.

From a corner, a bishop can only sweep seven. In addition, the hostile armies stand directly opposite and not diagonal to each other. As a rule, whoever exchanges a rook for a bishop or knight is making a bad deal. He loses "quality," in chess language.

The rook's real domain, however, is endgame play, for he is most likely to have a green light then. Among amateurs, the endgame is not very popular, for it is correctly considered tortuous and, much less correctly, boring. Rook endings are the trickiest and, annoyingly, the most common type of endgame play. They necessitate a polished technique, which, however, can be learned, as opposed to imaginative middle game combinations. Part of the curriculum is the pressure to place the rooks behind the passed pawns, one's own as well as the opponent's.

The rook-passed-pawn mnemonic is a good point at which to remember Siegbert Tarrasch, who was a chess intructor in Berlin for many years. He was a great teacher, the greatest, when pedagogical skill is ranked as highly as technical competence. Tarrasch had cheerful students by the thousands, and not only in Germany. "One did certain things," wrote the American critic Harold C. Schonberg, "because Dr. Tarrasch

Left: *Java, wood, circa 1880.*

Below, from left to right:
Germany, Meissen porcelain, designed 1752/53.
Portugal, porcelain, 20th century.
French-African, ivory, mid 19th century.
Russia, wood, decorated in color (Greek Orthodox Church), 20th century.

said one had to." Even national socialist chess fans learned much of what they were able to accomplish on the board from this Jew, who was called "Praeceptor Germaniae" without irony, who practiced medicine in Nuremberg and had the good fortune of dying peacefully in his bed in 1934, one year after Hitler came to power.

Taking advantage of an open line, installing an outpost in enemy territory, discovering a weak spot, a target of attack: these are some of the many things Tarrasch taught his readers. Above all, he tirelessly impressed them that attacking with empty hands was a terrible blunder, that what mattered most was developing an orderly formation so that the desired combination could

be carried out on a sound foundation. That strategy was not entirely new, as other masters condescendingly told the public, but Tarrasch had the gift of giving like no other. He may have had a sharp tongue, but his patience was enormous and his spirit benevolent. His unconventional suggestions, such as to fathom the endgame first, then to explore the middle game and not until the last to study openings, are certainly worth consideration. The enthusiastic response of Tarrasch's followers would certainly have failed to materialize had he not reaped success after success during his best time as a player. Later failures were occasionally due to his abhorrence of cramped, involved close formations, for his aversion

was combined with underestimation. Those who supported Nimzowitsch called Tarrasch dogmatic, a description that was more suited to Tarrasch's critics than to Tarrasch. International grand master Max Euwe compared the Praeceptor's style to "first class ready-to-wear clothing." Furthermore, Euwe accused Tarrasch of seeing only the rules and not the many exceptions. Well, yes, but others must have seen the exceptions even less frequently, for they stumbled more often and never could have gone so far as the brilliant Tarrasch, who lost a tournament to International grand master Lasker. Tarrasch, who could not stand Lasker, greeted him before the first round with the remark that he had only two words to tell him: check and mate. That was unfriendly but concise, for with the exception of these two words, a player was supposed to remain silent during the game. Tarrasch was hard on himself. After a tournament that had been rather unfruitful for him in San Sebastián, Spain, he was asked if he were going to indulge in "a few days of Babylon on the Seine" on his way home. Tarrasch rejected the pleasing idea of a detour through Paris for the marvelous reason that "I have to punish myself." That was a typical of him as the superb sentence with which he introduced his textbook: "Chess, like love, like music, has the capacity to make people happy."

The bishop's disadvantage is its limited movement. A bishop on a white square, no matter how fond of travelling, will never set foot on a black square. Never will its twin on black, no matter how boisterous, stray onto a light square. Both of them limit their enterprises to 32 squares, that is, one-half of the board. No other

THE BISHOP

Bishop: Scandinavian, bone (walrus), circa 1200.

nobleman is so honest. Whether a piece crawls like the king, scurries like the queen, hops like a knight or charges like a rook; whether it needs one move or 12 to accomplish its goal, it has the right to occupy any square. Only a single bishop provides what many people long for: absolute, 100 percent safety in certain places.

At the beginning of a game, each side has one bishop on a dark-colored square and one on a light square. Neither a businessman and his partner nor a tenor and soprano, not even a husband and wife, complement each other as well as the bishop pair. On that account, many players try to hold on to it. Therefore, it is more highly regarded than the other minor pair, the knights.

The bishop pair is comprised of the king's and the queen's bishops.

Bishop: India, ivory, early 19th century.

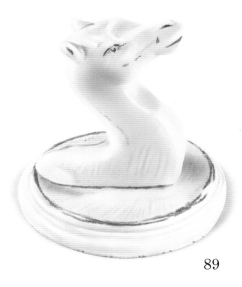

Scandinavian, carved from antler, 11th/12th century.

Below, from left to right:
Anglo-Saxon, whalebone, 10th century.
Germany, bone, 12th century.
Israel, soapstone, 20th century.
Ecuador, Tagua nutwood, 20th century.

Although seen dynamically the pair consists of a "good" and a "bad" bishop, which has nothing to do with strength, and even less with morals. The good twin has more freedom of movement, the bad twin less. The measure of this freedom is one's own pawns. A bishop may in an emergency capture an enemy pawn that was limiting its freedom of movement, whereas it may not do so with its own pawns. In certain openings, a pawn blocks the bishop's diagonal, thus promptly making this bishop bad. The bishop's terror is a chain of pawns in which one link provides cover for the next, something possible only on the diagonal. The exchange of a bad bishop is a small triumph for its player, insofar as his adversary has surrendered a well-developed light piece, possibly even his good bishop, and perhaps also believes in his ignorance that the exchange was equal.

Like the queen, the bishop was rejuvenated at the beginning of modern times.

Whereas formerly it had been allowed only a short jump to the next square on the diagonal, since the 15th century it has been the skewed figure that we know and love, and has become the most important building block of so-called Indian Defences, although the bishop itself has been completely Europeanized. It is reasoned that if movement on the diagonal is to be allowed at all, then the bishop is strongest on the longest one, which stretches from

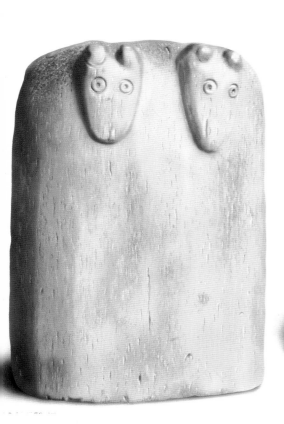

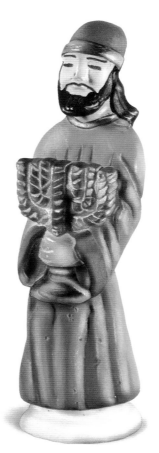

*Danish or German, bone (walrus),
13th century. The bishop is seated on
a throne in the cathedral. His eye
sockets were originally set with precious jewels.*

*Left: Germany, the bishop in his
pontifical robes mounted on a horse,
ivory 14th century.*

the corner adjoining the bishop to the diagonally opposite one. In the King's Indian Defence, it is the black king's bishop, and in the Queen's Indian Defence it is the black queen's bishop, that is steered onto the long diagonal. This is called a "fianchetto." In chess jargon that is being placed on the flank (wing), and is as little Indian as "Mitra" or "fool's cap." A "Fianchetto" is reminiscent of Italy, an old chess land, where the bishop bears the name *"alfiere,"* or flag-bearer. Etymologists, however, do not think of a flag, but of an Indian elephant in ancient Arabia. The elephant can be considered either a heavy-weight and thus a rook, or a tusk-bearer and thus a bishop. According to one theory, these two categories of pachyderms

were mixed up at one point — a reasonable theory, for why should the history of chess not have been as chaotic at one time as world history has always been? A second theory is that makers of chessmen kept designing the tusks longer until nobody knew what they had originally been modeled on; the English guessed it was a bishop's miter and the French thought it was a fool's cap. Staunton bishops have a notch that could just as well symbolize the embrasure of a castle.

Danish, ivory, late 12th – early 13th century.

In German, the bishop is called a "runner" (*Läufer*); in French, flatteringly, a "fool" (*fou*). The court jester was often the member of the court with the sharpest mind and the sassiest tongue. Other persons also had freedom of speech, as long as they uttered words that rang sweetly in the ruler's ears. Only the jester could contribute less charming remarks without risking the head on which his cap was perched.

The knight is the imp of the chessmen. The other pieces possess a certain stubbornness for all their speed: they always move in a perfectly straight line, even on the diagonal. With its move, however, the knight turns aside sharply because it has the privilege of jumping over the other men. The scope of this right was not fully recognized until the 20th century when complicated, cramped close formations were no longer despised but respected and even praised by some theorists. When facing a mass of pawns all wedged together, queens, bishops and rooks are

THE KNIGHT

stopped in mid-flight by the wall. The knight spies a free spot behind the pawn front and takes the wall as if it were a hurdle. Formerly, the knight was ranked a bit below a bishop, which suited the widespread preference for open lines and diagonals, whose length that knight cannot exploit. However, the knight is well-equipped to be an advance guard. Such an intruder, which costs the opponent no end of trouble to expel and which another piece, perhaps even the second knight, stands ready to replace, is annoying to the opponent. If the white knight

Knight, Arabian-Egyptian, rock crystal, between late 9th and early 11th century.

Left: *Bishop, England, ivory, from a set of Chessmen given by King James II to Samuel Pepys (1633 – 1703).*

95

in this setting, even though they are more of an attraction than the crowns of the kings, the trailing robes of the queens, the headgear of the bishops or the flails of the pawns. The nags are simply too large. That they are more voluminous than their riders and grooms may be acceptable, but that they visually overwhelm the poor queen goes against the spirit of the game. Large head, small brain, as an Italian proverb goes.

Now as ever, expertise and a feast for the eyes constitute the charm of "living chess." One April afternoon in 1988, two of the three best grand masters, Karpov and Timman, contributed the line of play on one of the most beautiful squares in the world, the "Grand Place" in Brussels. While they usually enter tournament halls on foot, they came to the game table in a coach amidst the applause of the curious onlookers. Fanfares resounded. Strategy and tactics became choreography. Karpov and Timman thought up the moves, and members of the "La Monnaie" theater carried them out. The 64 squares between the players were the usual chess-board, although much larger. Only half of the squares were painted, as the original dark grey color of the cobblestones was dark enough for the black squares. The two players wore street clothes, the "executive bodies" wore marvelous robes of white and black. The queens, one blond, the other brunette, were just as remarkable as the men were, yet not as large as one might have wished for the game, despite their

settles on e5 or the black on e4, a battle in the war can be considered won.

A nasty saying has it that thinking should be left to the horses, for they have larger heads. Among the creatures that became chess pieces, only the horse retained its characteristic head with Staunton. Where have the physiognomies of the kings and runners, the bishops and fools gone? Where are those of the 16 pawns or of the two queens, whose beauty might also have been captured in wood? In "living chess," when a game is dramatized on a life-sized chess-board with 32 people, the realism that was lost by the stylization of the pieces returns, whether the game is replayed or created by two masters at the time of play. However, real horses are a nuisance

Jewish, ivory, 18th century.

Right page, above:
Danish, ceramic, 20th century.

Below, from left to right:
Danish, ceramic, 20th century.
Portugal, porcelain, 20th century.
France (Dieppe), ivory, first half of the 19th century.
Czechoslovakia, polychrome porcelain, 20th century.
India, wood topped with ivory, 19th century.
Germany, Meissen porcelain, designed 1752/53.
Ecuador, Tagua nutwood, 20th century.
England, ivory, from a chess set given to Samuel Pepys by King James II (1633 – 1703).

ruffs above and their trains below. The kings bore small crowns on their heads, the pawns spears in their hands, and the bishops crossbows under their arms. The rooks were of cardboard, each "occupied" by a person who moved them when necessary. It is not difficult to guess what the horses looked life; of course, two were white and two black.

One of the tiny wooden pieces had hardly been moved by a grand master's hand before an official dressed in period clothes announced the move to the public and to the theater troupe over a microphone. A master of ceremonies then walked with measured steps to the figure involved and led it to another square or, if it had been captured, to the dressing rooms. Each time a piece was taken, five brass players clothed in imaginative historical costumes blared away from the balcony of City Hall. Karpov (Black) and Timman obligingly conceived a succession of very lively moves, in which many men were captured and the white and black horses together with their riders and pages could be set in motion often. The match ended after 20 moves, or about an hour, in a draw, which smelled a bit like a prior agreement among colleagues. Not always have such sensational events ended so peace-

fully by arbitration on the "Grand Place."

Almost exactly on the spot where Timman and Karpov considered their next moves, Counts Hoorne and Egmont were beheaded in 1568, victims of Spanish politics during the uprising of the Netherlands. In earlier centuries, the end of the living chess pieces was also cruel. Some despots, lords over life and death, had the poor devils who had embodied a captured piece executed on the spot. The intent of conceiving pawns and noblemen as people of flesh and blood was reduced to absurdity in disgusting ways. The battle of thoughts was degraded to mass murder. This brutality certainly increased the excitement of the game and led some sick souls to play chess. Not only sultans had their whims. It is claimed that a 16th century Russian czar, Ivan the Terrible, was among those who practised chess atrocities. Yet the rules of chess only offered blood-thirsty potentates an excuse; if the royal game had not existed, their dirty imaginations would have seized on other opportunities. The assumption that the atrocities were the "bloody consequence" of chess is an insult to the game. No wooden pawn is destroyed just because it disappears from the board. It may lie unnoticed next to a coffee cup, be thrown into a packing box and thor-

oughly shaken up during transport, but it is virtually certain that it will be used in the next game.

Of all the pieces waiting to be reused, the knight is not only the most striking, but also the most generic. Yet as individual pieces, untrained eyes do not always identify them correctly at first glance. The rook with its merlons is more likely to be recognized. But only the knight, even if it stands alone, is immediately seen for what it really denotes. It is unmistakable.

Above: *France, ivory, late 18th – early 19th century.*

Right: *Scandinavian, bone (walrus), circa 1200.*

Below, left and right: *Russian, walrus, 18th century.* *India, ivory, early 19th century.*

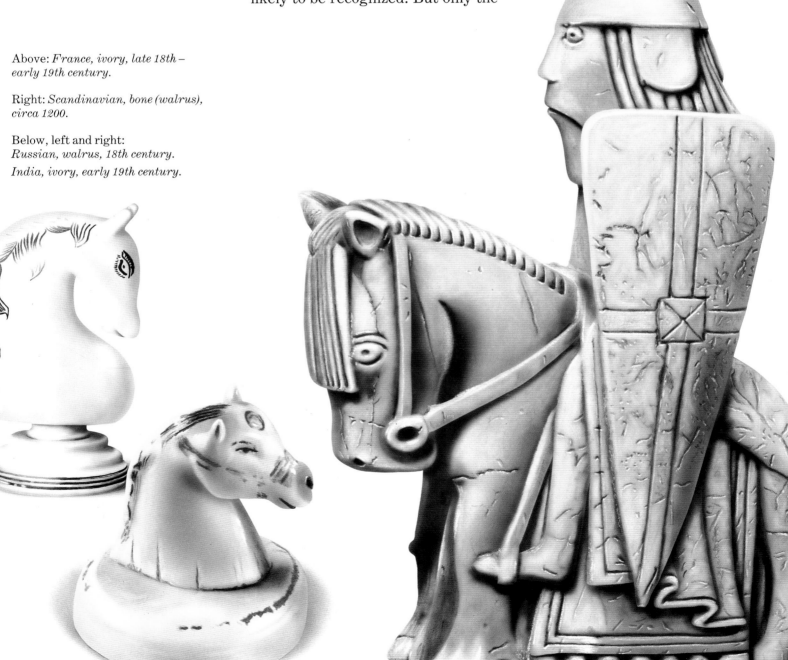

The commander of the white army still has the freedom of choice; the first move has not yet been made. In the second move, White will already have to consider Black's first response, as early as the third, perhaps even be forced into accepting an unpleasant variation. Yet at the beginning, White holds his fate in his own hands. Immediately before the first round of a world championship match, which hundreds watch live on the spot and millions follow closely via the media,

THE PAWN

an atmosphere of festive suspense arises. Will White move the king's or the queen's pawn? The audience may know the challenger's preference for one of the two opening moves but must take into account that the other may be chosen for the sake of surprise. Or will White move the queen's bishop's pawn? He surely won't want to indulge in extravagances such as the single step of the queen's rook's pawn, even though this eccentric opening has sometimes been followed by a happy end elsewhere. The single advance of the king's knight's pawn is also a possibility. One of the oldest games on record, dating from the 10th century, starts with that move, if the king's knight himself does not start

the action. In addition to the eight pawns, the rules also provide for the two knights being able to set off the game. Probably, however, White will reach for a middle pawn and if so, very likely move it two squares forward.

This double advance, which each pawn is allowed once and once only on its first more, was invented in the Middle Ages. Lay people and experts give different reasons for that, although both are correct. The layman sees a stimulation of vitality in this permission to advance, the expert a recognition of the strategic necessity of bringing the four squares in the middle of the board under control as quickly as possible. Myriads of thoughts in chess have concentrated on this center. In the hour of inner development, when a player loses the innocence of the practised beginner, he comprehends the unique meaning of the center, which is the geometric as well as the energetic middle. To become an expert, a player must learn that his position is in danger of falling apart if support in the center is lost, that a flank attack can be successful only if the center is secure (or at least blocked and barricaded), and that an impertinence by the opponent on one of the wings is most effectively chastised by activity in the center. A test question for pupils: "Why is 1 a3 not recommended?" The answer has to be, "For strategic reasons; the center is being neglected."

The battle for the center starts with the first move. For that reason, the masters of the 19th cen-

India, wood topped with ivory, 19th century.

Below, left and right:
Israel, soapstone (steatite), 20th century.
Java, wood, circa 1880.

Burma, painted wood, early 19th century.

Below, left and right:
Alpine Germany, painted wood, late 18th century.
Alpine Germany, painted wood, early 19th century.

tury, who knew or suspected that chess is more than just capturing and being captured, deliberately filled the center with pawns. In the first third of the 20th century came the "revolution."

People entertain diffuse notions of revolution, yet chess players saw an unparalleled upheaval in the new doctrine that the center need not be occupied by pawns from the beginning. Were great theorists such as Aaron Nimzowitsch and Richard Réti turning things upside down? Had our idols Capablanca and Alekhine let their heads be turned when they held back their center pawns? Was Tarrasch, who as a practical man experimented with the unorthodox openings now and then, not correct when he ran his hands through his hair?

In retrospect, the "revolution" was at most only half a revolution. Nimzowitsch and Réti preached consideration of the center with the same verve as every classical theorist. They had merely discovered the fine difference between occupying and controlling. They had realized that an army could command a few squares without being there in person. They endeavored to bring the center under control by fianchettoing the bishops, resulting in their being lined up to face the middle like cannons. The other pieces, from the cross-eyed knights to the multi-purpose queen, were positioned in promising perspectives. Let the opponent spread out his pawns in the center! His position would be undermined sooner or later and his fate sealed by drawing

up one's own center pawns. These pawns should remain quietly on the waiting list in the expectation of grand, or at least new, deployments.

The pawn stands in the fourth rank after the first opening moves. Of course, he has the innate tendency to proceed forward on his march. This is a tricky decision for the player because should the pawn venture far ahead early, he has the handicap of not being able to turn around. Pawn moves are difficult to repair. A forward queen can take to flight; an audacious knight can turn homeward contritely. Portable chessboards have a crack between the fourth and fifth ranks. That is the pawn's Rubicon. If it crosses over, it will be treated as an intruder. It is symptomatic that from its forward position, it has permission to once and never again capture en passant an adjoining adverse pawn that has just carried out the double advance, thus landing in the sixth rank, for that is where it wants to go anyway. At least, the opponent must reckon with that desire and prepare the necessary preventive measures. That, in turn, makes the pawn's next move an enormous risk that must be weighed carefully. If the step is chanced, Black is not to be taken lightly. The pawn is now treated with a respectful aversion, because its promotion to queen is in the offing. The pawn has now acquired a value that makes it advisable for its owner to rate its need for protection more highly than its forward drive. However, in an auspicious moment, the latter

Ecuador, Tagua nutwood, 20th century.

will prevail, and the pawn will stand in the seventh rank. Pawn? Both sides already treat it like a prospective queen, the pledge of victory for one, the guarantee of defeat for the other, because the pawn only needs to move or to capture a piece one more time. Of course, each adversary now does everything possible either to promote or eliminate the pawn, but finally the metamorphosis happens, the favorite event of players and moralists, in practice the acquisition of a queen for the price of a pawn.

Medieval authors intent on moral applications did well to dedicate several essays to the transformation of the least valuable man into the most versatile piece. Finally, for once, the comparison of chess to life was not so farfetched. The increase in strength is unique, for according to the measure of exchange a queen is worth at least eight pawns. Alfonso the Wise, a chess philosopher and King of Castile, stated in the *Codex,* published in 1283, that queening is symbolic of the ascent of a person from a lower to a higher standing. Jacobo da Cessole, the Dominican friar, wrote that no one should look down on the pawns, the *populares* among whom craftsmen, doctors, and merchants were counted, because they could attain the highest worldly or spiritual dominion through virtue (*virtutibus*). The reader, seeing himself transformed into the emperor or pope, can hold his breath. On the chessboard, every pawn without exception can be queened, but in the theater of life not all "little people,"

no matter how strongly they may be marked by *virtutibus,* have such opportunity. To continue this sobering point of view, what can be done with a man who has reached the other side of the board and is not allowed to turn around, other than to queen it? The only other conceivable rule would be for the pawn to make an exit without substitution after asserting itself, resulting, however, in a complete alteration of the game of chess. Not only would the pawn disappear, but also the player's motivation to get him to the last rank in view of great difficulties. Promotion is a systematic part of the game. By the way, in certain rare cases it is advisable to have the pawn promoted not to a queen, but to a knight, who is able to pose threats forbidden to the queen. Promotion to a rook or bishop is allowed, yet pointless, because anything they can do, the queen can do better.

It is possible to tell whether the pawn, of "foot-soldier," as it was called for years, carries the marshal's baton in its knapsack, to speak good Napoleonese. A simple consideration suffices for the time being to determine the pawn's chances of success. A pawn, like any other man, needs cover. Since it is uneconomical to use a stronger figure to protect a weaker one, a pawn should, if possible, be covered by its like. An "isolated" pawn, a pawn

Bottom: *Nuremberg, gilded bronze, circa 1570.*

Above: *France, ivory, first half of the 19th century.*

Opposite: *A Spanish set, hand-painted wood, 20th century.*

Below: *Czechoslovakia, porcelain, 20th century.*

> "In my opinion, the pawn has a soul,
> just like a person, wishes that lie dormant
> and unrecognized, and fears whose existence
> he himself hardly suspects."
>
> *Aaron Nimzowitsch*

without a next man, lives dangerously and is considered weak. An excellent, self-conceived formation is necessary for the pawn, led by a master's hand, before it can become a small trump. The situation of a pawn left behind after its two neighbors have stormed ahead is not very rosy. The other two cannot come to its aid because they are not allowed to move backwards. The "slow pawn" may catch up later, but at the moment it, too, is weak. The situation is similar for the pawn pair, not to mention a chain of three pawns. There, one pawn backs up the other, but unfortunately only in the choreographic and not in the charitable sense. The pawn pair must try to change itself into two adjoining men, something only possible when one of them can capture other pieces. The perfect example of a strong pawn is the passed pawn, characterized by the absence of hostile neighbors. Other pawns cannot approch it from the front or the side. In order to capture or even to block it, noblemen must appear, which increases its reputation and ties down opposing forces. Even stronger is the covered passed pawn (covered by another pawn). The completely connected passed pawns take turns advancing and covering gradually forcing the opponent to sacrifice a piece. If the enemy king is at a comfortable distance, one can speak of the ultimate in industrious pawns, the distant passed pawn.

Whereas a queen sacrifice is a strong spice everyone likes, a pawn sacrifice is an exquisitely ·delicate one that enraptures the connoisseur. The intended loss of a pawn (the unintended one is not worth talking about) may improve the formation by precisely the small amount that decides the battle of two equal minds.

Such a midget whose removal is inadvisable even though the opportunity is at hand bears the technical term "poisoned pawn." Players who take what they can get, who seize as many pawns as possible, must think of their own health, for the little pawns are also the toadstools of chess. Since little people can spoil so much on the board, the opera composer François André Philidor wrote a sentence in the mid-18th century that has outlived many of his works, yet still sounds like music to the inner ears of sensitive chess enthusiasts, "The pawns are the soul of chess."

THE BOARD AND THE SQUARES

Miniature and text from the manuscript written by Jacobo da Cessole (1407). Bavarian State Library, Munich.
"The knight on the chess-board must be mounted on his horse in a complete suit of armor. His horse should be covered with a caparison."

Opposite: *A wood and ceramic German board. One side is a chess-board, the other a backgammon board. The ceramic chess squares are decorated with painted hearts, bells, plant motifs and stylized figures, as well as with lucky numbers and figures from Tarot cards. Early 17th century.*

Everyone knows what a chessboard looks like, even though not everybody is in a position to lay it down correctly offhand, namely, with a light square at the lower righthand corner. Beginners often see nothing more in the well-known checkerboard pattern, frequently used in handicrafts, than a suitable base for pawns and pieces. Only when a player has matured will he pay sufficiently close attention to the board itself. He will recognize a field of force that changes in the course of a game. The center, ranks, and files are where they have always been, yet they suddenly become contributors to the game. One day, the player's gaze will perceive not only light and dark, but also strong and weak squares. The player will experience weak posts, which come and go, although sometimes at an excruciatingly slow pace, as open wounds in which the seed of destruction can sprout most easily. Weaknesses can arise in the simplest manner through one's own moves. Although a set of moves may have been aimed at a particular goal, which is enough, they may have also neglected the previous formation. The careful, defensive style of some masters can be explained by this flip side of the coin. There is no adequate judgement of a formation without consideration of the squares firmly in the hands of the player as well as of those over which he has lost control. The references to a cut-off point, important to the plot of Nabokov's novel *Lushin's Defence*, show that the writer knew how to

“Chess is a sport.
A violent sport ...
If it’s anything at all,
then it’s a fight.”

Marcel Duchamp

express himself in technically correct terms. He did not describe the formation, as another author might have done, but mentioned a weak pawn on f4 and a weakness of the opponent on d3.

If, when f4 is mentioned, two black diagonals running from c1 to h6 and h2 to b8 appear before the mind’s eye and, in addition, d3 is immediately identified as a light square that can be threatened by a knight on c5 or a bishop on a6, then the board is firmly anchored in one’s mind. The use of a small Roman letter and an Arabic numeral to designate squares is a convention observed even by the players used to writing in the Cyrillic alphabet. Of course, other methods are also conceivable, such as the two-numeral designation for squares used in long-distance chess, for example, 55 for e5 and 74 for g4, or a pure letter combination of one consonant and vowel each, formerly used in transmitting moves telegraphically. Each type of notation denotes not only the square, but also the move, and the ideal is represented by extreme shortness and absolute clarity. In the past, “1. e2 – e4” was written, and sometimes is still done so today. However, the e pawn’s double advance can be abbreviated to 1. e4, for what man could reach e4 on the first move other than the king’s pawn? In contrast to the pawns, noblemen are honored by indicating their initials according to the mother tongue of the player or publisher. “C” can denote the same piece as “S” or “N,” namely knight: in French *cheval, i.e.* horse, in German *Springer, i.e.,* jumper, whereby in English the knight suffers the misfortune of having to relinquish his first letter to the king and make do with the second. An accommodation can be made to an international audience by using symbols instead of numbers. Only in the cases of knights and rooks are there ambiguities that must be avoided. Rd5 is not sufficiently clear if both rooks, one on a5 and the other on d8, could reach d5. If the major piece on d8 is meant, Rdd5 or R8d5 must be written.

Algebraic notation is gradually winning out over the descriptive, which used to be customary in Anglo-Saxon countries. There, 1. e4 was designated as P – K4. The pawn

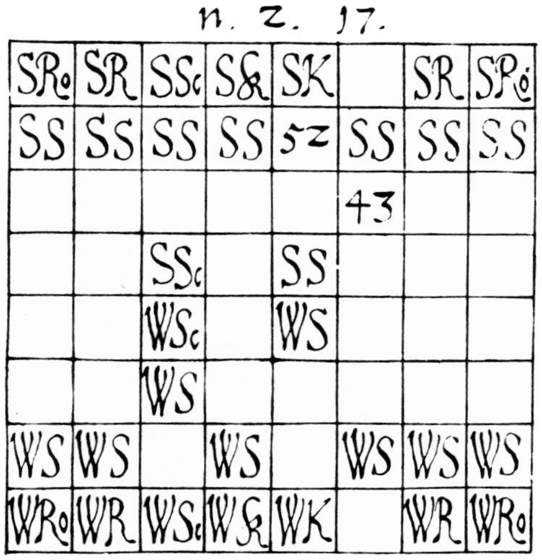

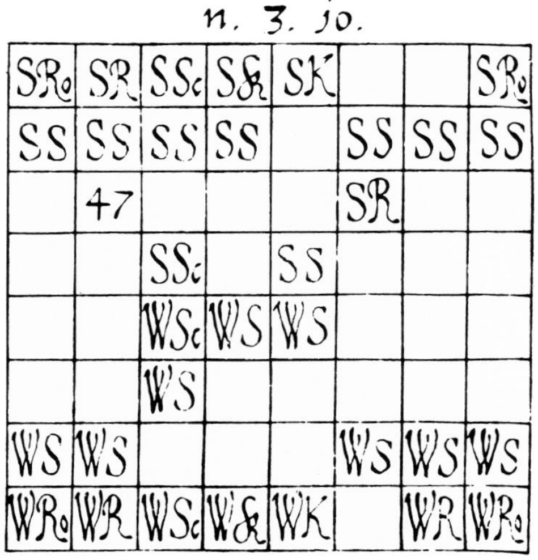

The Arabs not only wanted to defeat their opponents at chess, but also wanted to record their opponent’s chess moves. In order to do so, the individual chess fields had to be marked in such a way as to be clearly recognizable, or the moves themselves had to be clearly described. In “Selenus” the squares were numbered from 1 to 64. Pictured here are two games from Selenus’ chess book.

The game known as "Great Chess." A miniature from the chess book of Alfonso the Wise. This alternative to the classical game was played with several pieces on a 12 by 12 board.

moved to the fourth square of the king's file. The difference between the two systems of notation was based less on the dissimilarity of prose and mathematics than on the contrast between two perspectives: the descriptive notation is based on the chessmen, their original position

and the algebraic on the board. Algebraic notation indicates where the train is going, but also tells how the tracks run.

Chess was not always limited to a quadrilateral board or a certain number of squares. Long ago, the Byzantines played on a round board

Margrave Otto IV of Brandenburg playing chess. A miniature from the Manesse song manuscript by a miniaturist from the Upper Rhine. Early 14th century. Heidelberg, University Library, Pal. Germ. 848.

divided into circles and sectors. In 19th century England, four-person chess was considered a way to pass the time, and a Four-Hands Chess Club existed in London. Each of the

likes opponents, and not partners. Chess, a game free of coincidence, should not be turned into a game of chance through the unpredictability of allied spirits. The vulnerability of one's own psyche suffices completely for any competitor.

The player's gaze drills itself into the board. His chin and the tip of his nose often float above the squares as if he could increase his concentration by lowering his head.

four players had 16 men. As in bridge, the players sitting opposite each other are partners. This sometimes led to a type of resurrection, because it was possible to continue playing after one had been mated, if one's partner helped the defeated king out of its muddle. One wonders why four-handed chess fell out of favor. Probably, a chess player only

The wide world beyond the edges of the board sinks into oblivion. It is considered improper for that world to make itself noticeable — for a noise to intrudes into the shielded consciousness of the pondering player. It is the responsibility of tournament organizers to create conditions that allow players to concentrate on the 64 square micro-

cosmos. The chess mind is self-sufficient and respects the artificial enclosure of the large quadrilateral. No a9 or i1 squares exist. Thoughts do not drift or fly off into other rooms, they revolve around a small area. Not only the knight, but all chessmen, even all considerations, exercise themselves on this one surface like horses in a paddock.

The outer world has come to a standstill, shrouded in silence. Perhaps it refreshes the player with a cup of coffee, yet it must not distract him. There is no chess without the board, no chess thoughts without the picture of the checkered pattern, for the board is more than just a game board, it creates an intellectual space.

Chess-board and box, Eger (Bohemia), circa 1700. Various woods, 11.7 × 54.0 × 54.0 cm. The profiled frame is stained black and varnished and has punch work decoration in the form of flower tendrils and heraldic emblems. The chess-board has light and dark brown squares, inlaid with flowers and green-stained leaves. Inside the box is a backgammon board with inlaid dolphins and cartridge balls. On the reverse is an inlaid relief picturing a battle scene during the Turkish wars. Iron lock.

Right, from top to bottom:

Section of an ivory and ebony Spanish board. Moorish inlay of flowers alternating with white, green and brown squares. 16th century.

Chess-board inlaid with light and dark wood, decorated with flowers. Eger (Bohemia), 17th century.

Chess-board with mother-of-pearl and ebony squares. The black squares are decorated with gold and the whole board is edged with abstract ornamentation. The border has an ivory strip. The decoration reflects the influence of Asia Minor. 16th century.

Chess squares of fruitwood on a backgammon and chess-board. Carved work in various light and dark woods with rosettes and naturalistic floral motifs. Mid to late 17th century.

"Play is separated from normal life by its place and its length," wrote the Dutch historian Johan Huizinga, "it contains its course and its meaning in itself." In his famous book, *Homo ludens,* published in 1938, he does not write of chess, nor even of the characteristics of games, but of the influence of play itself on human culture. Nonetheless, what the chess player basically does and what his state of mind is are excellently described. Huizinga endeavored to get the nature of games. He thought that people are at liberty to indulge themselves in play or to leave it alone. "Play is not

Right: *Section of a German ceramic chess-board with painted flowers, hearts and figures. Early 17th century.*

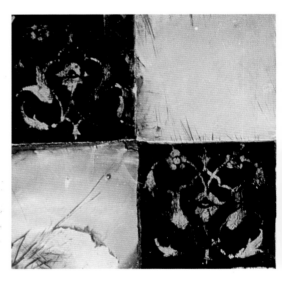

the usual, or actual, life." Play is beyond the normal processes of life, it interrupts them. In contrast to other, more or less necessary activities, play — this "intermezzo in daily life" — enchants by being superfluous and unrelated to the world's problems. Not that the player treats the game lightly. On the contrary,

he dedicates himself to it with an earnestness that is lacking in other activities more important for his mortal existence here on earth. The superfluity of play is precisely what makes it indispensable for a person who longs for relaxation and, in addition, a system free of the traces and weight of this world. "Play introduces a temporary, limited perfection into the imperfect world and perplexing life." The price of this perfection, however, is isolation, marked by the edge of the chess-board.

Indigenous to a "sphere above that of the purely biological pro-

cesses of feeding, reproducing and protecting oneself," play is attractive for the strictness of its rules. The French writer Paul Valéry maintained that scepticism was impossible with regard to game rules. And, Huizinga, the author of *Homo ludens,* adds "as soon as the rules are disobeyed, the game world col-

lapses. Then the sport is over." Hence the word "spoilsport." Huizinga points out that the spoilsport is something other than a cheater,

who at least pretends to play by the rules. A swindler would be lost in the world of chess. How could he possibly cheat? That is possible in card games, but not in chess, which by nature is played with an "open hand." It is conceivable that one of the adversaries secretly and quietly gives an unfavorably located rook a

Below left: *Chess squares inlaid with bone and engraved with fruit and leaf motifs. The squares are edged with engraved bone slivers. Southern Germany, 1560–1580.*

Amber chess-board, probably from Germany, with various portrayals of kings, queens, bishops and knights. A drawer is built into the board. 18th century.

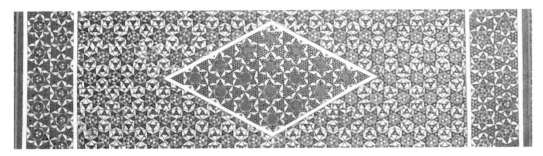

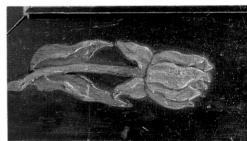

Game board and box, made in Vienna circa 1730. The squares used for chess and nine men's morris are on the outside. The inside was used for the backgammon game.

little push, or surreptitiously replaces a captured pawn on the board, but the mere mention of such a possibility comes close to being an insult. Any experienced player will

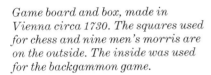

Above: *A detail of the border of a Persian chess-board, wood inlaid with ivory, Shiraz mosaic, circa 1900.*

Above right: *A detail of the border of a fruitwood game box showing the chess side. From Eger (Bohemia), 17th century.*

have noticed the positions well enough to be able to identify a change immediately, even after returning from the lavatory. He would at least be suspicious if the position of a man suddenly no longer corresponded to his previous calculations. Each adversary, each onlooker watches out that the rules are obeyed – even the general public does, in the case of games that are published after-

wards. No control could be stricter or easier. This is exactly the point where chess differs from real life. There are enough rules, regulations, and laws in the world, and people also observe them, yet not with the one-hundred-percent reliability that marks any chess player, who subjects himself to the inexorability of the unbendable rules of the game with a cheerful zeal. But in life? One

Left: *Chess-board with box, Austria (1872 – 1873). The black chessmen of the set are stained. The opposing kings are represented by Emperor Maximilian I, and King Ludwig XI of France. All the figures are dressed in historically correct, typical costumes. Maximilian has a breastplate beneath his cloak and the Golden Fleece around his neck. Ludwig XI also wears a breastplate beneath his cloak. Both are surrounded by their retinues. The bishops are Maximilian's field-marshals with the Hapsburg double-headed eagle on their cloaks. They are faced by their opponents, the French standard bearers. The knight; a rearing horse. The rook (castle); a Gothic tower rising above rocky crags and scrub. The pawns; infantry with halberds or muskets. The chess-board can be raised to store the figures. The chess set is rumored to have been found among the possessions of Emperor Franz Joseph of Austria.*

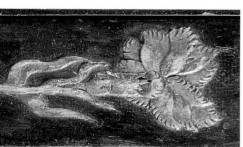

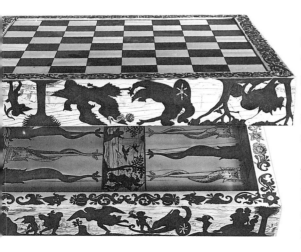

stretches a point, the next peers through his fingers, the third closes an eye, and the fourth takes the 11th Commandment to heart: thou shalt not let thyself be caught. In chess, everyone would be caught.

Yet aren't parallels constantly being drawn between chess and real life? Isn't chess thoroughly apt as a symbol of life precisely because of its diversity? The Yugoslavian

A detail of the border of a chess-board inlaid with mother-of-pearl and with gold decoration, 16th century.

Left: *Playing board, probably made in Augsburg (before 1700) from oak, ivory and tortoise shell. The edges are also richly ornamented with inlaid mythical scenes.*

115

> "A great many people have mastered the multiplication tables of chess nowadays and even know its logarithm tables by heart – therefore an attempt should occasionally be made to prove that two times two can also make five."
>
> *Mikail Tal*

Chess set and board, France circa 1870 – 1880. The faience board consists of white and cobalt blue squares, surrounded by ornamental borders worked in manganese red, cobalt blue, yellow and green.

Section of the decorative border.

duced such sentiments to simply "Chess is live."

In the beginning of his wonderful anthology *My 60 Memorable Games*, Fischer quotes Emanuel Lasker, who once wrote, "Well, lies and hypocrisy do not count for much on the chess boards of the masters," a self-evident statement that only has weight if it is understood as a sideswipe at life. Lies and hypocrisy

grand master Milan Vidmar called the game of chess a "well turned out miniature of life" in his autobiography *Golden Times of Chess*, well worth reading because not only is his own personality vividly captured, but also that of other famous chess players between 1900 and 1930. He asks, "Isn't nearly everything that real life requires contained in a chess battle: a spirit of enterprise, caution, courage, toughness, willpower, ambition and knowledge? After all, if one plays the game with seriousness, one experiences the highs and lows of success and failure over and over again. By playing chess over and over again, one can practice and learn the astonishingly realistic battle of life, even though it is in a reduced form." A world champion agrees with him in his book, *Garry Kasparov Teaches Chess*. "Like many other chess players, in the contest of chess I discover a surprisingly exact model of human life with its daily struggles and constant ups and downs." And, Bobby Fischer re-

Augsburg game board of ebony and horn. The exterior is a Chess game with portraits of kings and emperors. Circa 1600.

are the forces in the world! They would go to ruin on the 64 squares so real life is scarcely recognizable in chess just because of their absence. So how can Fischer say "Chess is life"? The upright Vidmar commented: "As soon as royal chess comes into contact with dirty money, it suddenly loses all, or at least a great part, of its enchantment." Today the leading and in many cases

Chess set and board, Germany (1925 – 1928), designed by Max Esser (1885 – 1943) for the State porcelain manufacturer Meissen. Both sets of figures are identical in shape with gold decoration, the white set being also trimmed in orange-red and the black set in dark grey.

Above left: *Wooden chess-board with inlaid ebony. Wooden chessmen.*

Above right: *Russian chess game with wood and ebony inlay. Chessmen of walrus bone.*

well-to-do grand masters could only sign their names under this sentence in an attack of hypocrisy: how can a "pleasant miniature of life" be created, if chess is so noble and money so filthy?

"You, dear friends, will never be successful anywhere if you do not develop in yourselves the perseverance, the diligence and the ability to estimate your potential objectively, to set yourselves realistic

Josip Broz Tito is pictured playing chess in 1944 at his partisan headquarters in a cave on the island of Vis. All his life he was an expert player and a lover of the chess game. The chess sets and figures pictured on these pages are samples from the collection in the Josip Broz Tito Memorial Center in Belgrade where his gifts from statesmen, public personalities and organizations from all over the world are displayed.

The answer has to be that some aspects of life and chess are comparable, yet fundamental differences remain. When Kasparov attributes such great expressiveness to the ups and downs, he might just as well compare the chess game to a roller coaster. In his textbook, he speaks to his readers directly:

goals and to pursue them consistently, decisively and actively." Every chess player would nod approvingly at this point. Others go quite far in life without these admirable qualities. Before a game starts, equal opportunity rules on the board. Where does it rule at the beginning of life's struggle? If at

this point someone should raise the objection that equal opportunity is also tarnished in chess, because White has the privilege of the first move, the response would be that many disadvantaged children would

The fact that chess players have always enjoyed such comparisons of chess to life, is due to the desire for intellectual loftiness that is particularly strong when one's own activity is subject to social or political

Above left: *Wooden chess-board and ivory pieces.*

Above right: *Peruvian chess game with a board made from rare woods, and chessmen of silver and gilded silver (black set).*

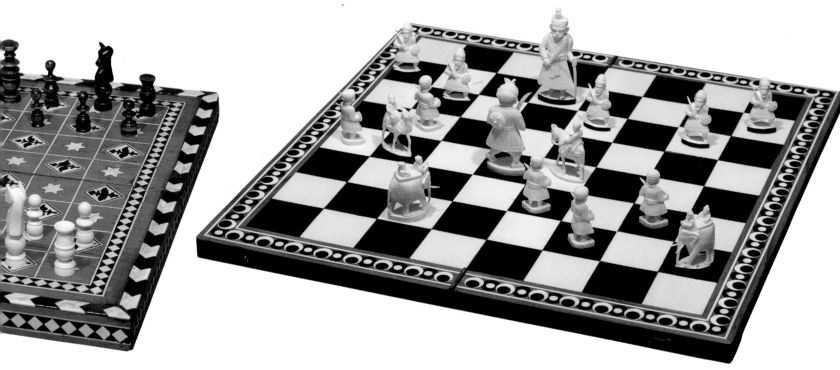

be happy if they only had to deal with such minor clouds. Instead, life sends one person into the arena with five rooks and another with other a single bishop. As compensation in real life, the law protects against the destructive urge that rages in chess.

ostracism. Chess has often been praised or even publicly supported, yet frequently also made light of, sometimes even directly forbidden. Today, chess can also stand some discriminating comparisons. A breath of comedy pervades chess clubs and tournament halls, for the players, especially the excellent ones, are sometimes considered

Chess-board and set of ivory chess figures. A gift from Indira Gandhi.

Above left: *Chess game used by Josip Broz Tito during the war years. The wooden board with inlaid ivory and ivory chessmen is also shown in Tito's photograph.*

> "Life is like a game
> of chess: we draw up a plan;
> this plan, however,
> is conditional on what
> – in chess, our opponent;
> in life our fate –
> will choose to do."
>
> *Arthur Schopenhauer*
> *in "Parerga and Paralipomena"*

A lady and cavalier playing chess.
Porcelain figure from Ludwigsburg
(around 1790).

Opposite: *Chess table with chessmen.*
Indian work from the 18th century.
This priceless little table of ebony
and bone served many purposes. It
has been preserved in superb condi-
tion.

odd, and sometimes actually are. Furthermore, it is generally known that several grand masters behave like big children in their free time. On the other hand, many intelligent, successful people can get along in their careers wonderfully without any knowledge of chess. Above all, any game has the reputation of being "only a game," *i.e.,* an affair whose importance cannot possibly compete with that of momentous happenings. For centuries, chess players had no idea what kind of glorification Friedrich Schiller would grant them one day with the astonishing declaration, "For, to put it frankly for once, man plays only when he is man in the full sense of the word, and he is a whole man only when he plays." It is remarkable that chess writers hesitate to quote this sentence. They would prefer to say that "that is too much praise." Schiller would not harbor a grudge against them, because he was not thinking of chess, but of art and aesthetics. Schiller's text might well be understood to say that the player makes it hard on himself; he has been spared the difficulties of life, but has exchanged them, voluntarily and confidently, for others.

The chess-board is an enclave, an oasis of order, a refuge for the human spirit. Whether it is decorated with gems or stained with dirt spots, it casts a unique, unforgettable spell on people. The game serves to "create relaxation for us and let us forget the cares of daily life for a moment." No health-resort director said that; it was Capablanca in his *Last Chess Lessons.*

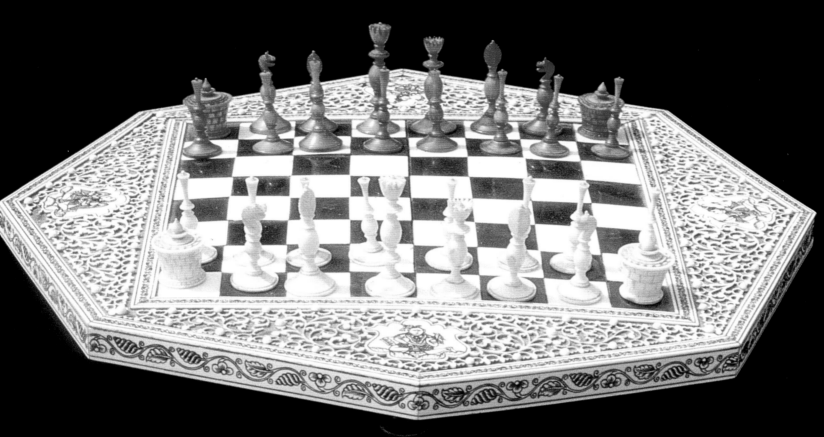

> "A combination is a series of moves (or a group of follow-up moves), during which both players make forced moves and which ends with an objective advantage for the active party."
>
> *Romanovsky*
> *in "The Middle Game"*

THE GAME ITSELF

Miniature and text from the hand-written manuscript (1407) by Jacobo da Cessole. Bavarian State Library, Munich.
"The fifth pawn should be placed in front of the queen and have the following form: he should sit on a master's stool with a book in his right hand and a tub or a box in his left. Tucked in his belt is a scalpel."

Chess arouses the passion that chains people to the board. The comparison of chess to an illness was once made by friendly Paul Keres when speaking of youth in general while also thinking about his own. The passion for chess usually befalls people still in their adolescent stages of development. It releases some of its victims when they approach high school graduation; some of them, however, it blesses and tortures their entire lives. Like a bacteria, the chess germ invades unexpectedly, perhaps during a harmless shuffling of pieces on the board, perhaps while looking at a position diagram. Sooner or later, the person infected by the germ becomes a bit strange. His viewpoint, broadened to understand the world, narrows to the study of chess. The beauty of combinational play lights up and outshines the other marvels of life. Chess partners are sought feverishly. A father may watch with great uneasiness as his son's hobby turns into a compulsion. The urge to play, by the way, is in its own way reasonable, because only long practice, including numerous defeats, leads to expertise. It is a vain hope that the mania will dissolve into nothing due to the relatively infrequent availability of a partner. For now, the power of imagination emerges. Even without a board and partner, the imagination incessantly concentrates on chess, during breakfast, on the way to school, during class, whenever and wherever it is possible. Soon, the books are discovered. For once it is

"I really believe that every chess player experiences a mixture of two esthetic pleasures: firstly, the abstract image, linked with the poetic idea of writing; secondly,

the rational pleasure of ideographically implementing this image on the chessboard. Not all artists may be chess players, but all chess players are artists."

Marcel Duchamp
in an address to the New York State Chess Federation in 1952

A watercolor of 1977 by André Miro titled "Chess Player on a Bench."

Eighty-two years of age separate young Walter Wisbey and graying Mr. Whiltard but they are united by their love of chess as pictured here in Cheltenham in August 1913. No one is too young and no one too old for chess — the only requirement is a clear head.

unnecessary to remind the student to kindly begin reading. The perusal of the literature is disturbingly intense and ends in bed, after midnight. Above all, theories of openings reveal their tempting charms. An arsenal opens, just the right preparation for future battles. During walks alone, the burning question is turned over and over in one's mind — which of the many openings are the most suitable, the most effective, in which opening systems is it worth specializing?

Chess nomenclature has grown over time and is remarkably unsystematic for a game that is so fascinating for its logic, among other things. Especially to lucid lay people, it is a puzzle that exactly "chooses" a certain opening, White or Black? And what does "choose" mean, anyway, since the opponent also has a say in the decision? It is difficult to reduce the matter to a simple formula, therefore, some explanation is required. If White plays 1.e4 or 1.d4, he is leaving the choice to Black, albeit a limited one. If Black loves the Grünfeld Defence and White begins play with 1.e4, Black has had bad luck, because the Grünfeld is only possible after 1.d4 or 1.c4, and not always even then. Black can respond to 1.e4 with 1.e5, and already the opening has a name, the Sicilian Defence. After 1.c6 or 1.e6, the name is also already determined: Caro-Kann or French. But what about 1.e5, the ancient, standard opening move? The baptism is delayed. If White answers with 2.Nf3, it is delayed further. If White had played 2.Nc3, one could speak of a Vienna Game, had he played 2.f4 it would have been a clear case of King's Gambit. Does Black control what happens to the opening after 2.Nf3? Yes and no: 2.d6 results in the Philidor Defence, 2.Nf6 in the Petrov, yet with the really excellent move 2.Nc6, everything remains open. It is possible that White will now play 3.d4 other 3.Bb5. Then the situation is evident, the opening is either the Scotch or the Ruy Lopez. However, if White wants to thumb his nose at the impatient beginner he will resort to 3.Nc3 and leave it to Black to make it a Three Knights Game with 3.Bb4 or a Four Knights Game with 3.Nf6. It is also possible that White decides to play 3.Bc4, by no means determining whether the Giuoco Piano (3.Bc5) or the Two Knights Game Deferred (3.Nf6) are emerging. Is that too complicated? The

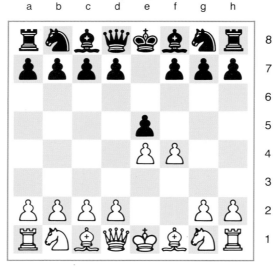

Left:
King's Gambit (Black to move): 1 e4 e5 2.f4.

Below: *The Queen's Gambit:*
1.d4 d5 2.c4 d5xc4.
This is hardly played nowadays in international tournaments.

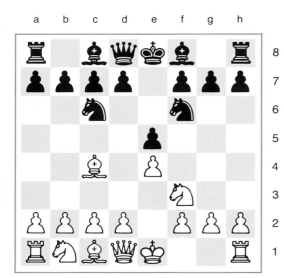

The two-knight game in next move (White to move):
1.e4 e5 2.Nf3 Nc6 3.Bc4 Nf6.

Right: *The three-knight game:*
1.e4 e5 2.Nf3 Nc6 3.Nc3 Bb4.

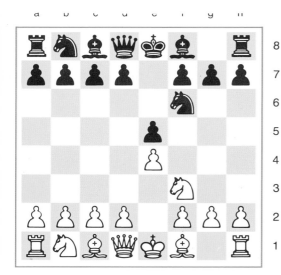

The Russian game or Petrov's game:
1.e4 e5 2.Nf3 Nf6.

phraseology is even more involved after 1.d4, because then variations are more plentiful than after 1.e4, allowing the final name to be given only after several moves.

Names of openings have diverse derivations. The designation "French Defence," for example, comes from a long-distance chess contest set in London and Paris during the 1830s. The London players made a move according to their custom, 1.e4, to which the Parisians responded with 1.e6, considered risky at that time, but the French won. Approximately 40 years later, the English had a lot of luck with 1.c4, which is why certain c4 openings are called "English." The "Ruy

Lopez" (called "Spanish" in German) is named for the Spaniard of the same name, because he introduced 3.Bb5. A definitive claim to originality can hardly ever be made anyway, as the estimated number of unknown variations in chess is large.

Once in a while, a player who wants to lure his opponent into unexplored territory will think up a nameless opening. There is a label for those, too, "irregular."

A Hungarian, Emil Gelenczei, analyzed the expansiveness of game openings in his book *200 Opening Traps:* "Therefore, what is irregular? A bad move that has not yet been proved a good one." That describes

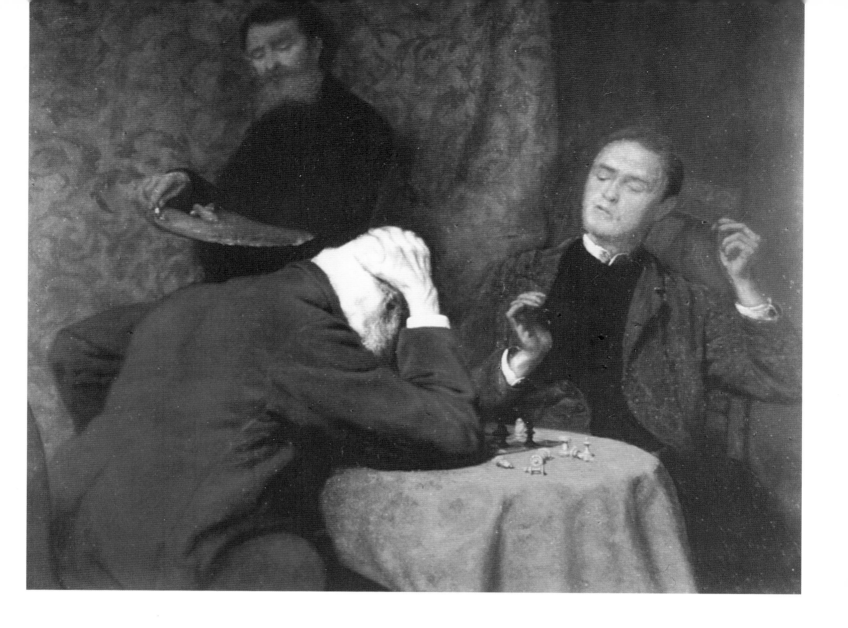

Alekhine's Defence, 1.e4 Nf6, perfectly. Black's first move was considered a miserable one, until Alekhine played it successfully one day. Then it was only considered daring, soon after, perfectly normal.

Not every name is adopted. The Germans wanted to rename the awkward "Two Knights Game Deferred" the "Prussian Defence," but the whole world was against them. Other names are smuggled in, hardly anyone knows from where. The "Pirć Opening" (1.e4 d6) was suddenly called the "Ufimtsev Opening" under Soviet influence, although Ufimtsev was completely unknown throughout the world, in contrast to the famous Yugoslavian grand master Pirć. The way in which these variations, also called systems, branch off and work the advanced middle game is astonishing, yet not unusual for an orderly, well-planned opening. Consider the Closed Ruy Lopez. It is not characterized by the second or third move, but by the ninth: the move 9 h3 literally speaks volumes, for entire books, not just a few pages, have been written about the consequences of this outside pawn move.

Grand masters know the tricks, at least the most important ones. Although they may have five hours time for 40 moves, some players are finished with the first 16 moves in

An oil painting of 1885, "The Chess Player," by the French artist Henri-Eugène Campan.

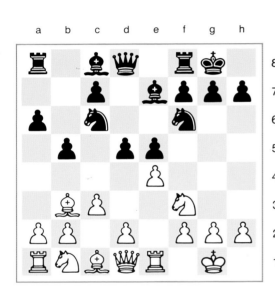

The Marshall attack (White to move):
1.e4 e5 2.Nf3 Nc6 3.Bb5 a6 4.Ba4 Nf6
5.0-0 Be7 6.Be1 b5 7.Bb3 0-0 8.c3 d5.

10 minutes, still a considerable amount of time, because they could rattle off the moves in their sleep. But what happens when Black avoids that ninth move by introducing Marshall's Counter-Attack? Then, a knowledge of theory pays off handsomely. Frank Marshall, a daredevil from the United States, had no idea what he would trigger with his attack; the most detailed studies have been made of the situation at the 24th or 28th move. The analysts did their job thoroughly. Many grand masters have perused the studies and absorbed them in such a way that it seems as if they had memorized them all. Perhaps some actually have. In any case, they lead the amateur to do so. It may be that they warn the amateur against learning by heart, but they induce him to do it anyway by proudly presenting their mastery of the most involved games. The warnings are justified. A player who "knows" a variation, but has not thought it through, resembles a parrot. He will have the unpleasant experience that his poor head is not equal to the variation he has been able to recall. The misery of many inexperienced players is due to their inability to solve the problems they themselves have posed by setting up such complicated formations. The German grand master, Wolfgang Unzicker, was correct in trying to deter beginners from choosing the more demanding variations in his textbook. "They are poison," he wrote.

A short example of how to deal with openings intellectually: con-

sider 1.d4 N.f6 2.c4 e6. 3.Nc4. That is a famous series of moves tested thousands of times, the beginning of the Nimzowitsch Defence. Why 1. ... Nf6? To prevent 2.e4, which would give White a strong center. Why 2. ... e6? To open the file for the king's bishop. Why 3.Nc3? To carry out e4 despite the black knight. Why 3. ... Bb4? To pin the white knight in order to thwart the double advance of the king's pawn once again. That should suffice. Only one thing more should be mentioned, that both sides must continue to play in the "spirit of the opening." White should never stop endeavoring to somehow get his king's pawn to e4; Black should not tire of putting an end to that. And each side should watch for the moment when other compensations are adequate to let him break off the contest for e4.

In the first half of the century, eminent authorities like Lasker and Capablanca allowed themselves a certain nonchalance in their treatment of openings. They knew they had what it takes to create exciting middle games from simple, uncomplicated openings. In the meantime, general principles of openings were preached to amateurs. They were taught how to develop as many chessmen and to win as much territory as they could in as few moves as possible. That is a reasonable lesson, although it has by now lost its exclusive validity. Common sense dictates that a chessman requires a certain minimum mobility to be effective. At the beginning of a game, the four rooks, for example, are

> "A good player is always lucky."
>
> *José Capablanca*
>
> "The loser is always at fault."
>
> *Vassily Panov*

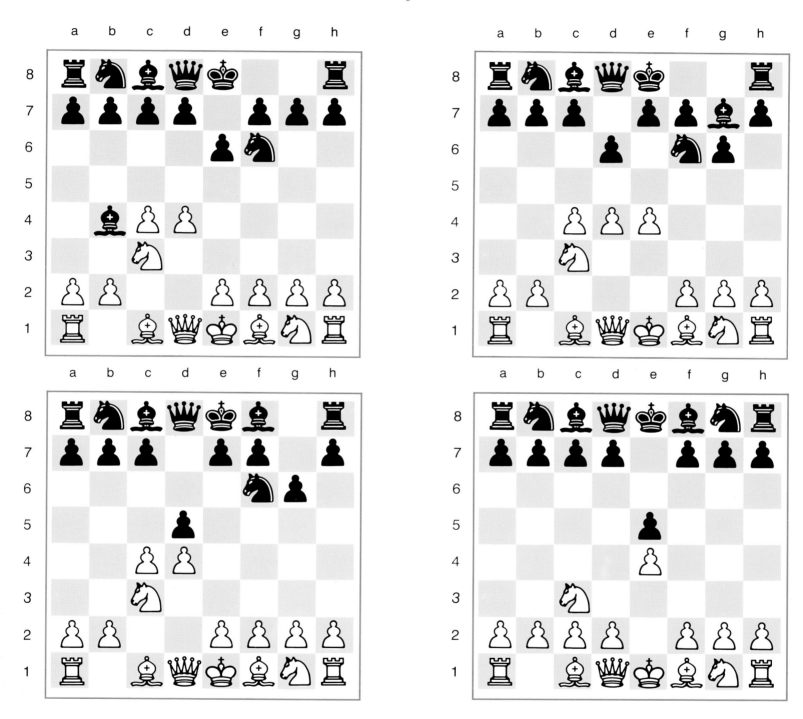

Above left: *The Nimzowitsch Indian defense (White to move): 1.d4 Nf6 2.c4 e6 3.Nc3 Bb4.*

Above right: *King's Indian (White to move): 1.d4 Nf6 2.c4 g6 3.Nc3 Bg7 4.e4 d6.*

Left: *Grünfeld Indian (White to move): 1.d4 Nf6 2.c4 g6 3.Nc3 d5.*

Right: *The Vienna game (Black to move): 1.e4 e5 2.Nc3.*

129

"Nature gave us the chess-board,
which we neither can nor will get out of;
Nature carved the pieces,
whose value, movement and ability gradually become familiar;

deadwood, as are the four bishops. These principles, like most, have been a bit overused; for example, the recommendation to move the knight and then the bishop, or the advice to move each man only once during the opening game. These were rules of thumb that soon became discredited due to the brilliant successes of those who disobeyed them. However, the wonderful days when these sayings only had to be observed loosely are gone.

International master Alekhine, a giant of chess, still made jokes about "Lady Theory." But the next international master, the Dutchman Euwe, wed the lady by undertaking the mammoth enterprise of writing a polished theory of openings in several volumes. Other authors also did themselves proud, enabling the chess fan to fill entire shelves with literature about openings. With each passing year, the theories became more involved and the learning of them more arduous. The method often thought to be scientific was a rather simple one; the results of years were reviewed, classified and examined for efficiency, theory as crystallized practice. The results were tested and either confirmed, modified or thrown on the scrap heap, only to be retrieved under certain circumstances. It is a lively circle: theory influences untiring practice, the latter, in turn, modifies theory.

Max Euwe from Holland, World Champion from 1935 to 1937 was a keen practitioner and system player. In his standard work entitled The Middle Game *he even incorporated human inadequacies into a system. One chapter dealt with greed, a second with deception, a third with sloth and a fourth with its opposite, indecision.*

Opposite: *"The Chess Game," an oil painting of the late 19th century. This historical painting depicts monks playing chess. Chess was already widespread in the monasteries during the Middle Ages. Even though it was repeatedly banned by the Church, its popularity was never suppressed.*

then it's up to us to make moves
from which we expect success;
each person tries this in his own way
and doesn't like others to interfere."

Goethe in "Schrift zur Naturwissenschaft"

Too much literature about openings is read; about the endgame too little. It is not that there is a lack of advocates speaking warmly of the endgame. However, the promise that the unique character of the chessmen will show up best when the board has largely been cleared does not make endgame study more attractive. Endgame technique is

A contest in the Café Kerkau in Berlin which, nevertheless, could not be called a coffee-house contest, because the two men sitting at the round table in 1909 were Akiba Rubinstein and Jacques Mieses who were definitely not amateurs. We can be sure that in this contest no mercy would be shown, not because of the audience but because of the demonstration board in the background.

difficult part of the theoretical treatment of middle games is its systematization, because middle game formations are the richest in nuances and their planning is the most intricate. Nevertheless, there are useful books on the subject, for example, the one by Euwe, who was interested in both theory and practice. Replay is especially popular; that is, repeating wonderful master games at home. But it is not worth duplicating a game if it is more a finger exercise than intellectual training. If the lay person endeavors to fathom at least a third of the thoughts that both original players entertained, discarded or carried out, he can be satisfied with himself.

Opposite: *In the Parisian "Café de la Régence" all kinds of games were played; chess, checkers, dominoes, billiards and cards. The café opened at eight in the morning and within a few hours the air was dense with smoke. It was a social advantage to be seen there which is why the café was frequented even by philosophers like Rousseau and Voltaire and also by politicians like Napoleon. Contemporary picture.*

considered dry, and thus the average amateur avoids it utterly. This dislike is strengthened by the observation that countless games, and not the worst ones, are decided in the middle game. But does the thirst for knowledge concentrate on the middle game? Not with the vehemence aimed at openings. The most

their thoughts and place no value on externals. Since they do not have much to say to each other verbally and demand from their surroundings only that they are not disturbed, the atmosphere becomes gloomier from hour to hour. It may smell of tobacco smoke and unaired clothing, and because barkeepers do

Left: *Between 1750 and 1830 anyone who wanted to play chess in Paris made his way to the Café de la Régence. There he would meet other amateur players like himself, but could also meet a professional player specifically hired for this purpose, who would play against anyone who asked and who could play. Such exceptional Master players as Pierre Saint-Amant, Charles La Bourdonnais, Alexandre Deschapelles and Lionel Kieseritzky were all to be found here in the service of gastronomy. Contemporary picture.*

When the German philosopher *Gottfried Wilhelm Leibnitz* was once asked what use the game of chess was, he replied that it served as "Practice in the ability to think and innovate. Wherever we have to make use of reason, we need an elaborate method to reach our goals. And moreover: a person's resourcefulness is most apparent when playing."

Does the royal game still appear royal to the impartial guest who enters a chess club? Nobody likes to generalize. Yet the places the beginner will seek out sooner or later in search of congenial souls, that is, opponents, rarely boast an attractive, elegant atmosphere. Chess players are completely engrossed in not like people who run up small bills but sit around for a long time, they make the least attractive room, if any, available to their chess-playing guests. Hardly any alcohol flows; strong liquor is seen as a hindrance to strong combinations. There is no room to serve food, because the chessboard lies in the

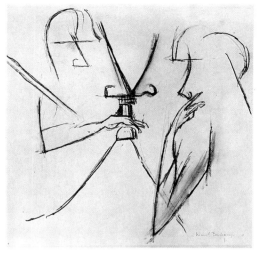

Right: *Two opponents and their joint opponent, the chess clock. A study by Marcel Duchamp, it is one of over 25 of his works on the subject of chess, which, considering what an enthusiastic player he was, is probably not a particularly large number.*

Chess clock, as used in private and public tournaments.

Right: *Several chess expressions have been adopted in the language of politicians, e.g. "a clever move," "stalemate" and "to hang a game." The flair of an intellectual is good for politics, where, after all, someone is always "on the move." Some political professionals are happy to be photographed at the chess-board. One evening in May 1976 in the State Chancellery in Bonn, Chancellor Helmut Schmidt and the future State President Richard von Weizsäcker together with other politicians played chess against a group of journalists.*

remarks about each move. This bad habit runs counter to the silence of tournament games.

space normally reserved for place setting.

Therefore, it is advisable for a chess club to find shelter in a place where no one is keen on large sales of liquor or food. Public or semi public institutions are suitable if they can provide quiet corners and a refrigerator for self-service.

Chess players may interrupt the silence themselves. They like to play speed chess, because otherwise their pace is markedly slow and they, like other people, go from one extreme to the other. In speed chess, as in tournaments, the chess timer is used, a double clock in which one clock starts to run as soon as the other has stopped. It is a measuring instrument that is indispensable for keeping track of the time both sides use for reflection. The first player to exceed his time loses, no matter how good or bad his position is. Since the time limit is usually five minutes for each side, the players, who must think up and make their moves in a flash, have no time to press the switch gently. On the contrary, they deal it blows whose loudness is excused by the speed of their hand movements. If an entire club is playing speed chess, it sounds like distant machine gun fire. Other characteristic noises come from the players who routinely make derogatory or encouraging

Usually, joining a club serves the development of self-awareness After three or four games with different opponents, one's weaknesses and strengths are no longer a secret. The pomposity of certain club members who sarcastically and contemptuously reproach anyone who cannot beat them is an incentive to improve performance. Yet one day, these members will be overtaken and not even noticed by those they wanted to humiliate.

Left: *When photographers were not present to record a scene the artists were happy to take their place. In this picture P. Wasiljev portrayed Gorki and Lenin and, looking on, Lenin's life companion Krupskaja.*

The club is essential for the aspiring player after other opportunities to test his intellectual prowess have been exhausted. Chess history boasts two strong-

holds. The first is the Café de la Régence in Paris around 1800 and the second is the Café Central in Vienna around 1900. In both coffee houses, demigods played against blunderers every day, for money, naturally. It was not a disgrace to earn one's bread in this manner, and even if it had been, the masters could not afford to pay attention to that. Many of them were beggars then. Money and gambling fever were among the reasons that the game had a bad re-

"The downfall of the King" is the title of this lithograph showing Napoleon, banned to St. Helena, at one of his favorite occupations. At that time many European kings had fallen and finally the French Emperor also succumbed. The fact that there was no Emperor in the chess set may have soothed the banished potentate, even though he had, in better times, called the "Game of Kings" the "Game of Emperors."

Left: *"The monkey has made his move." This satirical sketch by the German artist A. Paul Weber does not flatter chess enthusiasts. However, one often cannot choose one's opponent.*

> "Surely chess is a sad waste of brains."
>
> *Walter Scott*

> The slowness of genius is hard to bear, but the slowness of mediocrity is intolerable."
>
> *Henry Buckle*

The Chess Club in Belgrade is an international meeting place. Not only training according to strict criteria is carried out here, but also large-scale tournaments.

putation in the Middle Ages and was outlawed here and there. Even today, a master earns his money from people who seek out a contest despite their weaknesses, but many great players disdain waiting for customers in cafés and prefer to play simultaneous games. The better player compensates for the difference in ability by giving himself a handicap. Whereas the handicap in games for points consists of doing without a rook or knight, in this case it is the number of opponents. The master makes his rounds to the different opponents, stopping at each board only long enough to make his move; each of his adversaries can think in peace and quiet about his next move, to be carried out when the master returns. Nevertheless, most paying guests lose their games.

In Europe, careers can be made only through the clubs, the smallest unit in the system of regional and national associations, and finally, the World Chess Federation. The clubs or associations sponsor international tournaments, compete against each other and try to work their way up in the system. Known everywhere, because it is financially attractive, is the Deutsche Bundesliga (Federal German League), in which several prominent foreigners play, among them some who can barely speak three or four words of German. Each team is allowed to recruit two of its eight members from abroad. On the basis of a complicated mathematical evaluation, which counts not only the number of victories, but also the quality of the

defeated opponents, the internationally binding strength of each first class player is continually calculated. By fulfilling certain norms, highly talented players develop into grand masters. Every professional player longs for this title, which provides him with a ranking and

"The public views *Korchnoi* as an anarchist who wants to annihilate his opponent in broad daylight; *Kasparov* as a young Napoleon of chess, with extraordinarily heavy artillery; *Karpov*, however, is like a policeman, who would prefer to have his opponent handcuffed and chained and locked away behind bars."

Raymund Keene in "Chess" 1984

perhaps an income on which he can more or less survive.

Today, there are more than 200 grand masters in the world, the consequence of which is that hardly any other players, no matter how active, can count on the rather limited attention of a broad audience. The number of grand masters will continue to rise, because interest in

Stand still, look, make your move, walk on, stand still, look, move ... on November 9, 1985 Viktor Korchnoi played 40 opponents in Lucerne. Simultaneous exhibitions are a popular source of income among grand masters.

"A threat
is more effective than
the actual implementation."

Savielly Tartakover

He had more time but still he lost. It is annoying, but neither scratching his head nor his back is going to change anything. In simultaneous exhibitions the extremely busy master moving from table to table always plays with White.

chess is burgeoning everywhere. In addition, the average life span in industrialized countries in increasing and the coveted title is not revoked, even after inactivity due to advanced age. The enlargement of the hallowed circle now takes place chiefly mathematically (*i.e.*, correctly); the first nominations originated in the whim of a czar. In 1914, Nicholaus II, who had sponsored a tournament organized by the St. Petersburg Chess Association, graced the participants who had taken the first five places with the honorary title of "grand master"

at the tournament banquet. Out of a field including Dr. Ossip Bernstein, Akiba Rubenstein, Aaron Nimzowitsch, James Henry Blackburne, David Janovski and Isidor Gunsberg, the five who had really earned a spectacular distinction were Emanuel Lasker, José Raúl Capablanca, Siegbert Tarrasch, Alexander Alekhine and Frank Marshall. These were not just men who had played phenomenally well, these were the personification of ideals: Lasker stood for wisdom and psychology, Capablanca for harmony and unerring sureness, Tarrasch for methodology and exactness, Alekhine for originality and devilishness, Marshall for humor and slyness. The word "grand master" had already been commonly used to designate excellent masters before this date and continued to be loosely applied for awhile, as the present norms were not defined until after the Second World War. The Russians, who have produced more grand masters than any other country, have adopted the German word *"Großmeister"* into their language.

Grand masters lead a nomadic existence in the prime of their lives. They travel from tournament to tournament, if they receive permission, which is never certain in Eastern bloc countries. They are fed and lodged at the cost of the organizers and collect starting money, discreet donations and sometimes, also, a prize, which of course must be hard currency and not a silver trophy or pewter plate. Grand masters are well acquainted with each other, and if by coincidence two have not yet met, they know each other through word-of-mouth and from technical journals. They are accustomed to half-empty halls. In many countries, chess suffers from a lack of spectators. After all, sitting and thinking are activities that offer little spectacle. The fastest moves are made right at the beginning of a tournament round: the referee rushes from table to table starts the clocks with a hurried, yet well-aimed blow. Some participants are already present, others enter late, but all of them immediately give the impression of falling into a sort of trance. All the same, action during the opening is relatively brisk. Because the openings are memorized, move follows move, clock-stopping, clock-stopping, notation of the opponent's move, the notation of one's own move. Many an eccentric demonstrates brooding indecisiveness even before his very first move. That, however, is only playacting. These players have also thought things over for years and are now firmly decided to follow certain systems as White and

Left: *In 1914, Nicholas II extended the invitation to an international tournament in St. Petersburg. Five players reached the final round: Lasker, Capablanca, Alekhine, Tarrasch and Marshall. The Czar conferred on them the title of "Grand Masters".*

The British player Nigel Short was hardly older than his opponents when he played a simultaneous game against students in Hamburg. His international career had already begun when he was still a young child. Today he is among the world's elite. As with all those who have reached the top, he considers his ability to play simultaneous games as a matter of course.

"Like Tristan Tzara, I have the disadvantage
of always wanting to win.
A good chess player, however,
prefers a fine game to a victory."

Fernando Arrabal

Opposite, far right: *The battle takes place in their heads and also in the heads of the audience. The wild combinations, considered, cast aside, and maybe checked out again, cannot be fully mirrored in their faces, but their inner tension is easy to read. The onlooker is often twice as surprised as the individual player who, while knowing his own thoughts, does not know those of his opponent. Sometimes the tension is so great that one has the impression that a player should realize through mental telepathy what the audience is thinking for or against him (as in this picture of a simultaneous exhibition with Wolfgang Unzicker).*

Above and above right: *The simultaneous exhibition held in Lucerne in 1985 was a social event. Relatives, friends, club colleagues wanted to see how a certain player would perform, and crossed their fingers for one of the 40 players. However, many of them wanted to watch the grand master Korchnoi.*

as Black, depending on the opponent. Regardless of his retrievable repertoire of openings, he would like to let his adversary squirm a bit or perhaps even to find the inner quiet not automatically at hand. Soon, the transition to the middle game follows, placing the master under a moral obligation to think up a plan, because to play randomly and leave the initiative to his opponent is considered an unprofessional sin of omission. It takes a long time for a plan to be made and its feasibility examined, partly pedantically and partly prophetically. A chess fan who wants to follow a particular game needs great patience: The hall is silent; funerals are noisier. Every so often, a person in the audience whispers a combination into his neighbor's ear, a result of his im-

patience and desire to think along with the players. The neighbor refutes his idea. When the whispering reaches the ear of the referee, he restores quiet with an energetic gesture.

There have been notable exceptions to the usual silence of the chess match. In a report about the contest between Louis Charles Mahé de la Bourdonnais and Alexander McDonnell in London in 1834, George Walter described how the entire audience at the Westminster Chess Club gave unrestrained vent to its feelings. Everybody spoke their minds freely. La Bourdonnais, who would have become an international master, if such titles existed in his day, did not have command of the English that rang out around him. He was accustomed to noise and occasionally broke out in fits of laughter during the match. In another incident, Robert Hübner, a child of our times who wanted and needed quiet, was playing against Petrosyan in a candidates' tourna-

ment for the world championship. Noise coming from the streets of Sevilla filled the badly situated chess hall. The noise grated on Hübner's nerves, but did not bother his adversary, because Petrosyan, who was hard of hearing, simply turned off his hearing aid, something that had already paid off for him once against Mecking. Hübner broke off the game, thus losing it.

The plan does not seem to be completed yet. A few tables to the left, the players entrust the signed game (by Black and White) forms to the tournament organizers for safekeeping. From there, they are distributed to the press.

The player has two or two-and-a half hours for 40 moves and can allot it at his will. If he wastes a large part of it for his middle game plan, he must compensate by rushing later. Even if the game has not been decided after 40 moves and is adjourned until after dinner, it will last either four of five hours. The four-hour limit, to which clubs have always adhered in their contests, has been observed by the elite in their battles for only a short time. There was a period during which no limit was set. During the 18th and 19th centuries, for example, everyone thought for as long as he liked, and even if he were teased for it, it was still his move. Stories are told of players taking short naps and of a player whose turn it had been for two hours, but who had forgotten to move. It is hard to believe that an oaf like Mucklow in England simply did nothing until his stronger opponent had to go home and therefore

In some cases, the game of chess serves to satisfy adult fantasies. In others, it is an intellectual activity in different guises from which it differs in that it offers a greater prurient satisfaction than the activities normally pursued by an intellectual.

Reuben Fine

Right: *Bobby Fischer was always a gentleman at the chess-board. Of course he wanted to destroy — "to kill" — his opponent, but only by using his mental skill not by trickery. Wolfgang Unzicker once described his encounters with Fischer and confirmed the faultless manners of his superior grand master. There was no "enfant terrible" sitting behind the pawns and pieces — but a mature if not old master.*

Mikail Tal from Riga in Latvia took the title away from Botvinnik in 1960 only to hand it back in 1961. Tal only lost his reputation as a sorcerer many years later. The picture shows the 25-year-old ex-World Champion at the European Team Championships in Oberhausen.

Right: *Boris Spassky is a great master, a brilliant practitioner, rather lazy, and a man who has devoted himself to enjoying the pleasures of life.*

lost. While waiting his turn, the opponent in our hypothetical game is in the background, moving like a bird in a gilded cage. The background is an area from which the audience is bared, whether by ropes or a forestage. A separate buffet and individual lavatories may demonstrate the organizer's class. The opponent, tired of wandering, sits back down at the table, but soon, having had enough of sitting, gets up again. The opponent is by no means irritated because it is not his time that is elapsing.

The onlooker starts to think that his patience is foolish. He turns inwardly to the subject of the men's attire. The players are dressed casually to carelessly. The onlooker recalls a well-to-do grand master who came to play in ragged jeans and tennis shoes full of holes. During the first third of the century, when the Austrian Carl Schlechter perished of starvation and Emanuel Lasker debated whether he could not earn more money playing bridge, tournament participants' clothing was more correct, from standing collars to spats. The players attached great importance to gentlemanly appearance, despite their lack of financial means.

The plotter stretches himself a bit, but does not make a move. The twitch of his body did not escape our spectater only because he craves a change in the position. Several times already, he has thought that the player's right hand was reaching for a piece, whereas in reality the player was only reaching for his chin or the back of his head. The witness of world championship matches suffers the most from such unintended deceptions, because they are really only two individuals to watch — not a good dozen, as in many grand master tournaments. Who

"The Grand Masters only play
to the same rules, too,
but they know them better
than we do."

Andreas Dückstein

Left: *This is certainly no poker face. Wolfgang Unzicker is one of those who finds it very difficult to hide his inner thoughts. From the faces of such people it is easy to read the effort being made to appraise several alternatives, the doubts with which they seek a way out of a possibly hopeless position, but also the satisfaction with which they look forward to a favorable end to the game.*

The Armenian player Tigran Petrosyan — a chess player and a bit of an actor. He knows that those taking part in a tournament are on stage and are exposed to the open gaze of the public and, most of all, of their opponent. A little acting can therefore do no harm. What Petrosyan is really thinking about, nobody has been able to find out. Whatever the case may be, in Euwe's words "his patience is absolutely insurmountable."

"Nowadays we see chess as a sport,

will be the next holder of the title? The onlooker dwells on this question, which the occupies all chess fans. Suddenly he sees that the hesitant player finally makes a move on his game form. The opponent, who has never lost sight of the board, hurries over, looks for and discovers the change in a split-second, and writes it down in turn.

The result is not necessarily a revelation. Perhaps it is even a puzzle for the onlooker. The beginning of a far-reaching strategic enterprise creates a bit of confusion in untrained minds. Yet even old Miguel Najdorf, who commented the Meran world championship match between Karpov and Korchnoi in an adjoining room, did not comprehend a move despite visibly straining his grand master mind, tried to cover up his lack of comprehension with the remark "this is a strategic move." Actually, the unfathomable is either a mistake or the height of sophistication. For example, it could be that an attack on the queen's wing is being engineered. Alright, but the opponent will know how to intercept that by regourping his forces, as the onlooker will realize after strenuous consideration. This is exactly what is intended. Let the opponent keep the upper hand on the queen's side. For, while he is keeping it, three of the attacker's pieces are swinging over to the king's wing, left uncovered by the defense. Such are game plans in chess.

Do the players use other than purely intellectual means? Certainly! Millions of people play chess, and it would be abnormal if there

were not several black sheep among them. Tobacco smoke and garlic know how to make themselves obvious. Some people can chew noisily with empty mouths, others blow their noses incessantly without having a cold. However, grand masters strictly observe refined manners, not because of strict morals but out of fear of arousing the impression that they depend on histrionics. Nevertheless, during a match in Belgrade, Boris Spassky succeeded in making the audience laugh and his rival Victor Korchnoi exceedingly angry. On stage, where it was warm and not very bright, Spassky tried on two types of headgear, a woolen cap and a sunshade. Mikail Tal, the wizard of combinations, had a stare some adversaries found rather penetrating. One of them, Pal Benkö, an Hungarian who had fled to the United States in 1956, therefore wore sunglasses during the game. Tal, who was no slouch, also got himself a pair of dark glasses in an unusual style with oversized lenses, which enraged his opponent more than the looks had beforehand. A protest to the referee did not help. Benkö only registered the audience's laughter. In addition, Tal smoked. The time he took for contemplation could have been measured in cigarette lengths. Many chess players smoke while playing. Somehow, it seems to fit them (may health fanatics forgive this comment), but because it is a symbol of extreme inner tension when the cigarette ash, held upright, grows longer and longer without being knocked off, when the embers apa sport that stimulates the whole person.   *Willi Weyer*

proach the fingers within a pinch, so to speak, without anyone daring to make the grand master aware of the danger.

True grand master malice is the offer of a draw out of the blue. "Why," the opponent is supposed to ask, "is this guy offering me a draw right now, when I'm really going strong? Does he see something that

has escaped me? Nonsense. I'll refuse the offer. But if I refuse, then I will feel morally obligated to win. But if he gets angry at my refusal and plays better than before, can I beat him?"

Every tournament player endeavors to show a face no one can read. Yet body language is not silenced on demand. A player may be

The decisive moment. His opponent and the public may have been waiting for a long time. Is the player still free to choose? The rule states, "If it has been touched it must be moved." The chess piece that has been picked up must be moved even when the scales suddenly fall from a player's eyes and he sees that it would have been better to have picked up a different piece. However, he still has a choice of many squares on which to place his chessman. Thus his hesitation.

After the Second World War there was a lot of commotion about the "Soviet Chess School." Did it mean a building, or an institution or a doctrine? Soviet players said that it

Given the fact that Jan Timman was not Dutch but from Georgia or the Ukraine, he could boast of being a product of that school. Perhaps he really is. Worldwide, the big names learn from each other.

was a method. Is the school a figment of the imagination? This is not the answer either, for the education of talented young Soviet players is not left in their own hands. A group of grand masters, trainers and functionaries supervises their education. By the time the players first go abroad they are usually already very strong. This is what happened with Anatoly Karpov (below) and Artur Yusupov (above).

betrayed by his reddened earlobe, the furrow on his brow. Each grand master has his own personal way of glancing quickly and sharply at his adversary, as if by accident. Grand master Karpov had stolen several furtive, yet firm glances at his successor, Kasparov, when one day the latter collected himself and simulated a nervousness he by no means felt. These details remain hidden to the normal unlooker, who is struck by the cruder impression that the players, possessed by an evil spirit, could turn into pillars of salt. Stories, such as the one about the player who absentmindedly stirred his coffee with a bishop instead of a spoon are found in literature, but not in tournament halls.

Our spectator suddenly has the thrilling feeling that a sensational sequence is pending. On two other boards, victories have been recorded, still triumphs that do not interrupt the stubborn general silence. The players whose games have ended analyze their work playing through the games, trying out variations, suggesting alternatives in sign language. Behind our onlooker's back, a crowd is gathering. Once the game begins to come to a head, it is because the player's strategy has succeeded by and large, but the player is now terribly pressed for time. Six moves still have to be made before the small metal flag falls on the face of the clock. The minute hand has already started to lift the flag. The player does not have to write these six moves down anymore, as his opponent does, but only needs to check them off on his form; still, he needs to figure them out and carry them out correctly. There, the player makes a queen move. The opponent still has a relatively large amount of time, but a much worse situation. He has hardly moved when the response comes like a shot. The attacker needs a small eternity for his next move, five whole seconds, but then things happen in rapid succession. The 40th move is made just before the metal flag falls. Only two more moves, and the assailant has won. But the silence of the roll must

be maintained because other games are still in progress.

If a helpful soul had operated a demonstration board in the background and tried to duplicate the game with magnetic symbols, he could not have kept up at the end. That is the disadvantage of the demonstration board. The umbilical cord of electronics is better and more up to date. The piece placed on a square of the board sets off impulses, and the position appears as a diagram on a computer screen, either in the tournament hall or elsewhere.

Not only the eminent authorities, but also their cannon fodder take part in most large tournaments. However, the "Grand master Association," founded in 1988, has succeeded once again in keeping the crème de la crème to itself in its world cup tournaments. The games are not necessarily better for it. Beautiful chess cannot be had on demand, and the best precondition for its being produced to the joyful surprise of the audience still seems to be a pair of partners with a small, yet evident difference in capabilities. The candidate tournaments, which are the preliminary matches for the world championship challenge, the championship match itself, are no guarantee of stirring combinational play.

It takes two to play chess. Yet a custom has become popular by which the second partner's presence

is spared. He need only be reachable by mail and willing to correspond with his partner via preprinted cards. Grands may last for months at a time. The activity of postal chess is based on the loneliness of the thinker — its good reputation on the supposed thoroughness of his thoughts. In the office, on the bus, in the bathtub and in front of his bookshelves filled with chess literature, the postal player can hatch his next move at his leisure. The quality of postal play is, surprisingly, no more melancholic or rousing than direct chess. Furthermore, correspondence with several others must be maintained simultaneously in official tournaments. However that may be, the kiss of inspiration does not lend itself to being dispersed over time.

In 1770, a "mechanized" chess partner was presented by Baron Wolfgang von Kempelen at the court of Empress Maria Theresa. Von Kempelen created an "automatic chess machine" resembling a Turkish player, equipped with a decorative turban, sitting at a chessboard.

The automatic Turk beat every living Viennese player. In the box underneath the chess-board, rods, rollers, and wheels were open to view. However, thanks to several mirrors the people saw more parts than there really were. In fact there was enough

Do chess players even realize that they are smoking when they are smoking? The player's smoking pleasure is mostly subconscious. Boris Spassky (left) smoked a lot but not as much as Mikail Tal even though his health was not the best. Young Tal without a cigarette – a very unusual snapshot (middle). Only the ambitious young Icelandic player doesn't let off steam in the tournament hall. He is Johann Hjartarson (right).

Garry Kasparov's favorite word is "imagination." He is a World Champion who takes risks and plays aggressively, the sort of game the general public loves. Kasparov's speciality is the sacrifice of the pawn that allows him to take the initiative.

Mundus vult decipi — *the world wants to be deceived. The open door of the mechanical chess player allows everybody to see the cogs, wheels and screws, but at the last moment as the*

door is closed, a chess master is hidden in the cabinet. The colorful Turk is a marionette which gave its name to the Viennese Privy Councillor von Kempelen's mechanical chess player. "The Turk" was first presented in 1770 at the court of Empress Maria Theresa and thereafter was presented in many large cities in Europe as an opponent to be reckoned with.

space for an expert to guide the arm of the machine. As late as the 19th century, such hide-and-seek games were great sensations, because modern man very willingly allows himself to get excited over the possibility of his future dispensability.

Today, chess programs for computers have arrived on the scene. The suspicions raised by computerized chess were allayed by a British computer expert who said that mankind will not give up chess, just as it will not give up the hundred-meter race, although cars can drive more quickly. Nonetheless, many people want to know whether a computer will someday defeat the grand master. At the present, the best chess played by computers corresponds to that of a strong master, and soon computers will play grand master level chess. Yet even if at some point the machine should overwhelm the world champion, a hymn of praise to the human chess mind would still be due at the victory ceremony to the brain that so long and so tenaciously escaped the persecution of electronics. A clever person makes it easy on himself. Of the, let's say, 40 possibilities that arise in a certain middle-game situation, he will not pay the slightest attention to 30. Of the remaining 10, he will ignore 6 after brief reflection. He will give careful consideration to four possibilities, taking good care not to investigate all conceivable consequences. He will only calculate beyond a few moves if he senses that it is worth it, for he has intuition, experience and a feeling for positions. On the other hand, the computer does things the hard way; it calculated and calculates as if its life depended on it. No idea is so foolish that the computer will not pursue it. But let no one turn up his nose: diligence is not a bad substitute for talent.

Chess computers (as seen here in the picture "Mephisto") are excellent trainers. With amazing speed and an incorruptible lack of mercy they point out every tactical mistake. Their strength is the falsification of variations and analyses.

The tactician knows what he has to do, if there is something he can do; the strategist grasps what he has to do, when there is nothing to do. In the sense of this wise witticism, the computer is a brilliant tactician. Mating a king that has no chance left, or capturing a queen

The international Master David Levy is sitting in a television studio in Hamburg. The robot arm of his opponent, Chess 4.8, is maneuvered by a computer in the United States. Is this what mankind has to look forward to?

149

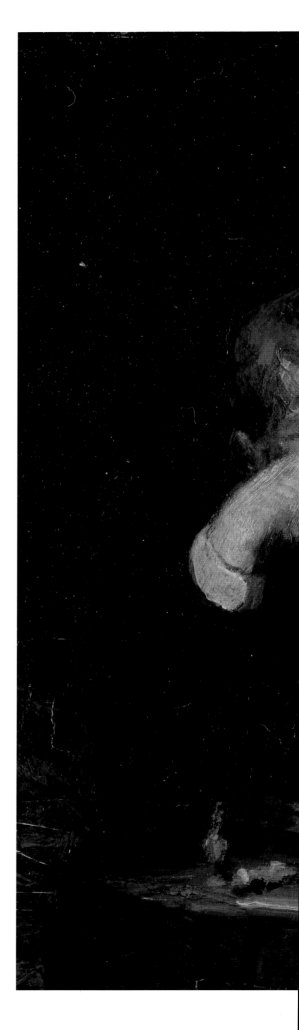

that is lost in any variation, the computer can do that in the twinkling of an eye. Pure solutions are its domain. It is in its element when confronted with the type of chess problems published in newspapers. In the absence of such problems, the computer shows a deficiency with respect to strategy. Yet in this area, also, the computer is advancing. The computer would be on the same level as homo sapiens if it managed to develop a plan that did justice to the position and was equal to the best possible defence similar to the one for which our spectator waited so long.

"Every chess player will confirm that the game of chess, this wondrous gift from the East, is not only the oldest and finest of all games, but, bordering on play, art and science, belongs to the greatest of spiritual delights."

Siegbert Tarrasch

151

KNIGHTS, CITIZENS, WOMEN

Miniature and text from the handwritten manuscript (1407) by Jacobo da Cessole. Bavarian State Library, Munich.
"The Rook (Tower) must be a mounted knight with a cloak made of pelts and a head covering also trimmed with pelts. In his right hand he should hold a small branch to indicate that he is the governor and the representative of the prince."

Opposite: The last page of the Alfonso the Wise chess book. A Christian knight and a Moslem are playing chess in a tent in front of which stand two lances. With a gesture of invitation the Moslem indicates a bottle and drinking cup.

The chessboard and ivory pieces hold the gaze of 14-year-old Tristan. He is a bright nobleman, a paragon in the best sense of the Middle Ages. He knows all there is to know: he can speak many languages, gallop with a loose rein, shoot an arrow through the flying mane of a runaway horse, hunt and train falcons, shoot and disembowel game. He has also taken a liking to chess; the inlaid board and the elaborately carved pieces interest him more than the ermine, walrus tusks, precious stones and other valuable cargo on the Norwegian trade ship anchored off the French coast. Unluckily for him the foreign traders are impressed with him. They compliment him and invite him to play a game of chess in the tent that they have set up on deck. Tristan concentrates, moves, ponders, duduces, racks his brains, attacks and mates his opponent with a queen's move. As he leans back, feeling satisfied, he notices waves splashing against the sides of the ship. The ship has sailed out of port. He has been kidnapped.

This is an episode from Richard Wagner's *Tristan and Isolde,* which has often been quoted. It is a wonderful description of the way in which a player can become so involved in a chess game that he is unaware of the outside world, throwing caution to the wind! *Tristan and Isolde* is not a chess story but a love story. In the epics of the Middle Ages, chess played a small but thoroughly remarkable role. Many poets were of the opinion that chess skill embellished a gentleman. They also

"It is too much of
a game for seriousness
and too much seriousness
for a game."

Gotthold Ephraim Lessing

Below: *Courtly love, hunting and chess filled the days of the knights. A scene from the* King Alfonso the Wise *chess book.*

thought that the game was an embellishment for a lady. Although high social prestige associated with chess in one thing, the frequency with which the game appears in daily life is another. Of all the cultural techniques for killing time and banishing boredom, chess has been seen as a particularly noble one. One should not, however, come to the conclusion that the knights made full use of this opportunity.

The knights, who were granted the honor of being the first

> "Improvement of the king,
> endeavor, the prevention of idleness
> and the training of farsighted,
> logical, mental enjoyment."
>
> *Jacobo da Cessole*
> *on the invention of chess*

Christian chess players, were armored riders whose usual seat was the saddle, not the chair. They were either feuding with one another or merely hanging around. The ideals of knighthood are based on physical exertion, not on mental activity. It was the duty of the knight to support those people who were weak and good, courageously and with self-sacrifice, and to do battle in the true sense of the word, for those who were unfairly persecuted. In chess, on the contrary, innocence does not come into play at all, and weakness is to be taken advantage of. Even so, the knights fulfilled two important conditions for the elevated practice of chess: they were well off and they had time. those who work the whole day and

fall into bed dog-tired do not play chess, except as a kind of narcotic. Chess requires spare time — the occasional freedom from serious problems and pressing duties, the forced leisure of the prisoner being an exception. Chess does not depend on a high standard of living. Standards of living are relative. By medieval standards of civilization, the standard of living of the knights was good; by our standards it was terrible.

In fact, the game of chess is more suited to the life of the monk than to that of the knight who is an outdoorsman. Among clerics, the permissibility of an activity involving castles and bishops was much disputed, not so much because the game was considered profane, but

Top row: *Miniatures from the Manesse manuscript which originated in Zurich around 1330/40. It portrays the distinguished poet Wolfram von Eschenbach, Tristan von Hamle, Walther von Klingen, and the Margrave Otto IV of Brandenburg who is playing chess with a lady. During the Middle Ages, chess was widespread and highly valued in the world of the courts. Women also played.*

155

Pope Innocent III (1198 – 1216) pictured in a mosaic which adorned the apse of the ancient Basilica of St. Peter in Rome. As a power-conscious and political Prince of the Church, he was one of the most prominent figures of the late Middle Ages.

The Dominican monk, Jacobo da Cessole, preached morality and taught chess — and managed to mix one with the other. His chess book became a best-seller for many generations and had to be copied by hand a thousand times. In 1458, Johann Pachmann from Amberg, a graduate of the University of Paris, sent this copy to the Elector Frederick von der Pfalz. A facsimile version of the original, which is kept in the Biblioteca Vatican, was published in 1988.

because of its link with money, for which it was generally played; also because fights broke out when gamblers allowed the mental combat to degenerate into the physical. Even so, Pope Innocent III, a giant among the leaders of the church, held chess in high enough regard to put his name on a well-known book on chess.

The most important literary work of this kind was written by a Dominican, the previously mentioned Jacobo da Cessole. The title of the work, *Moralities*, shows that in addition to the game, the author is concerned with human morality and the duties of the aristocracy. He also used chess as an occasion to discuss the duties of the bourgeois as

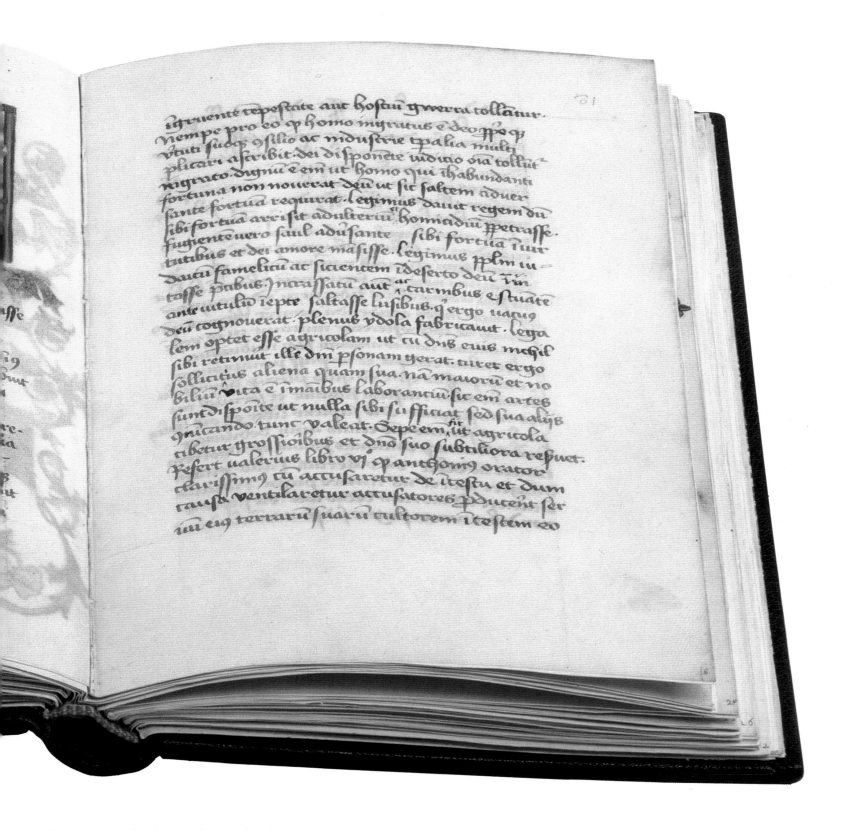

well, or example those of the physician. How is this possible? Simply in
that the physician is represented by
the queen's pawn. Brother Jacobo
had turned the pawns or foot
soldiers into representatives of the
professionals of the town. For example, the clothmaker, dyer, tailor
and furrier are on f2; the merchant
and money changer are on e2; the

physician or surgeon or pharmacist
are on d2. But why does the physician, of all pieces, stand in front of
the queen? Here is his answer given
in the original Latin: *"Ante reginam
vero medicus statuitur, ut casti-
tatem in corpore habere signitur."*
This is a typical argument: "The
physician stands in front of the
queen so that it is obvious that he is

On the left, the king seated on his throne holding the orb and scepter, and on the right, the queen. The ruling couple are at the top of the so-cial pyramid of the Middle Ages.

From the foreword to a German edition of the chess treatise by Gerhard F. Schmidt:

"We know with certainty that Jacobo came from Lombardy, but otherwise all we know of him is what he wrote about himself in the first chapter of his work. He was a preacher who developed the idea of using the game of chess to illustrate his sermons and to anchor his teachings more firmly in the minds of his listeners — the game of chess being generally well-known and very popular in the Middle Ages. He used the chess pieces and their positions in the game to illustrate the positions of the upper and lower classes (he excluded the clergy). The distribution and deployment of the figures on the chess board, and the arrangement of the chess board itself became the basis for a series of sermons tying together all manner of observations and teachings. He illustrated these sermons with numerous exemplary stories mostly taken from the classics, rarely using examples from Biblical or contemporary material. As an experienced teacher of morals he guarded against allowing zeal to become vituperation or bitter satire, or of tiring his faithful followers with long drawn out moral discourses, or of boring them at every turn with stories whose contents were generally known such as stories from the Bible or legends about the saints. This moderation and the cleverly calculated dissemination of his views, and the edifying and instructive stories together with the warnings which developed from them, and not least the actual contents of the stories, all contributed to the fact that his sermons were received so well that his fellow monks and his listeners begged him to write them down, thus making them available to other spiritual advisers who could then pass them on for the edification of the people. The actual literary and spiritual importance of this work probably lies in the choice of the sermons. Although they contain no hint of even a whisper of the Renaissance spirit, it is obvious that at the very least the sermons definitely carried certain views of pre-Christian classical antiquity to the general public and introduced heathen paragons of virtue to the faithful and encouraged them to imitate them.

Jacobo acceded to the requests of his fellow monks and wrote his work in the form of a latin treatise some time around 1275."

From left to right:

The judge (symbol of the bishop), the compatriot and the doctor (pawns).

Blacksmith and innkeeper (pawns).

The knight (miles, knight), wool craftsman and town gatekeeper (pawns).

The governor (rook), moneychanger and messenger (pawns).

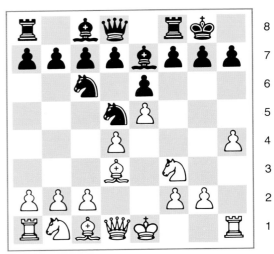

Grecos Mate:
1. Bxh7 + Kxh7 2.Ng5 + Kg6 (2.-Kg8 3.Qh5 f5
4.g6 follows mate; 2.-Bxg5 3.hxg5 + follows
mate.) 3. h5 + Kh6 4.Nxf7 + with win for the
queen.

A young courtier. A handsome man and, it can be assumed, a man skilled in the arts of chivalry, as for example, he has complete control over his horse and handles a bow and arrow with professional skill. From such a man society also expected good manners and the ability to spend his time in a manner appropriate to his social class, for example by playing chess. Painting by Gozzoli Benozzo (1420 – 1497).

chaste." When he examines the queen or other women, his chastity must be guaranteed. Jacobo advises him to read and to study a lot; he is not afraid, in this context, to repeat the common conviction that some physicians are closer to being murderers (*occisor hominum*) than medical doctors. It was the intention of the Dominican to pinpoint the grievances of his time. This becomes evident from some remarks he makes about the propensity of physicians to settle their differences of opinion, at the sickbed of all places. Nevertheless, the urge of the author to evoke ancient times is even stronger. Once, no one was successful in seducing the great, chaste Hippocrates, not even a beautiful prostitute, who to win a bet, lay down with him in bed. When she was laughed at for her failure, she defended herself by saying that she classified this exemplary physician as a statue, not a human being.

What do visits to the sick, diagnosis, Hippocrates and the prostitute have to do with the problems of the farmer? Absolutely nothing of course. Jacobo and his many readers knew that too, and amused themselves with such mental acrobatics all the more. Approval from all sides justified the use of this method of preaching morality in a chess book and teaching chess in a moral tract. Today, the cleric would have a harder time of it, as the public demands that one follow the laws of logic. The medieval mind inclined towards symbols and allegories, as well as towards the art of bringing dissimilar ideas together. Such things also appealed to the new social strata of townspeople. The rising bourgeoisie, which was not without imitative instincts, adopted the game of chess from the aristocracy. The bourgeoisie, especially northern Italians, was developing towards that which would be called the Renaissance, an epoch with new life styles and new ideals.

The ideal Renaissance man was the *uomo universale*, the true antipode of the 20th century European. The universal, that is the many-sided, all-around person, had to know more and be capable of more than Tristan. He had to be able to read and recite Latin texts as if they were Florentine ones; he had to feel at home in literature and science; and in the field of music he had to be a minor virtuoso. The appreciation of architecture, sculpture and painting were expected. So that these did not remain purely theoretical, he had to be able to show an art collection. Was that all? For heaven's sake no! The *uomo*

An anonymous Tuscan artist of the
15th century painted this picture
which is in strong contrast to the
peaceful game of chess. The setting is
the Florentine Davanzati Palace and
the title, "The Civettino Game". This
was a type of boxing match — one
boxer trod on the other's foot and
then they carried on with their fists.

161

universale could not be a stay-at-home. It was also required of him that he wrestles, jumps, swims, runs races, and rides and fences. Hence, a mixture of esthete and go-getter? Not at all, as such a mixture had not proved itself in society. The Renaissance man also had to be a kind of lounge lizard. Part of the versatility of this type was dependent on an inclination towards elegant, never dull, conversation, with

serious themes lightly delivered. Finally, the *uomo universale* was an excellent dancer. He, who was of the opinion that people could achieve whatever they set their minds to, would have punished the present day specialist, who uses his professional knowledge as an excuse for his ignorance in all other areas, with disdain. In any case, he would never have invited him to his home. He would have regarded

Part of a wall hanging from 1470, which pictured "The Garden of Love." The woman is portrayed as the Queen of Love. Love has played many a trick on chess. At a tournament in Hastings in 1962, a young American lady gave up her game after playing a few rounds saying that she was in love and could no longer concentrate on the game.

the French *honnete homme,* nor the English gentleman was morally or socially obliged to direct his attention to the royal game. It was not a necessity for any of these models or examples. It was required of the gentleman, the most recent in the sequence of types, to be fair. But one does not get anywhere by being fair in chess. Neither fairness nor unfairness find expression in the orderly game. Chess was never very fashionable, and that was to its advantage.

Chess has never made itself unpopular by being too closely associated with an epoch, a social strata or a state. If the game had spread because of a fashionable trend, it would soon have been branded as unfashionable. The 20th century looked down on the Romantic period, which in turn looked down on the Enlightenment, which in turn looked down on the Baroque. Things always have to move on, there always has to be something new; that is why the remark that the rules of chess are some hundred years old is not appropriate for advertising. In fact, the person who devotes himself to chess does not value its venerable age, but its eternal youth. Be honest: who wants to take part in medieval field games? Who wants to parrot what happened in the Café de la Régence? Not even historians put much value on ancient life styles. But no mold encircles the rules of chess. Even though they have passed through thousands and thousands of brains, they are still as fresh as the day on which they were invented.

many modern grand masters as barbarians. Should he play chess at all? Not necessarily. Dancing and Latin were more important. Even though the Renaissance man may have been a phantom many times over, whose living image was only a rough approximation of the ideal, it is nevertheless instructive that the ability to play chess was regarded as dispensable. Neither the Italian *cortigiano,* nor the Spanish *hidalgo,* nor

Chess is an impressive way of passing time. The medieval authors have already eulogized the entertainment that it creates. Apart from that, chess is a pleasure. Though the fun does not extend to the training and competitions of professionals, it nevertheless remains a game, the beauty and brilliance of which are satisfying in themselves. These are the qualities, which are in some places in danger of being inter-

preted negatively. In states in which activities of individuals are judged according to their social relevance, some spokesmen have been quick to make little of the entertainment value of the game, but on the other hand to extol its usefulness. It is not by chance that, especially in socialist countries, players and authors feel pressured to justify the game.

Continued on page 170

In Shakespeare's "Tempest," Ferdinand and Miranda play chess. The English painter E. Reginald Frampton, one of the last of the Pre-Raphaelites, recorded the scene on canvas.

In this cartoon Fred Marcus has suggested one of the many possible ways of disappointing a woman on her wedding night.

"Checkmate," a lithograph by Irwing Amen, 1977. The players' faces reflect the tension as the game draws to an end.

"What the public barely realizes is that the mental strain necessary for hard tournament chess takes a heavier toll on a player's physical fitness than athletic exercises. A doctor of good repute in Havana, whom I consulted during my last competition there, told me: 'I overdid things as an amateur, both at chess as well as in the gymnasium, and I cannot imagine anything that puts such a strain on all the vital organs – brain, heart, kidneys and liver – at once, as the excitement when playing chess in front of a critical audience'."

Wilhelm Steinitz

Following double page:
Contest in a coffee house in Trieste. What should he do? It is not the first time in his life that the elderly gentleman has had to answer the question of all questions. He knows all his weaknesses and the uncertainty of his position, but, whether he now wins or loses, tomorrow he will take up the battle again.

A club game in Moscow. What should he do? If this anonymous player were as skilled as the grand masters he idolizes, he could probably answer the question very quickly. Not only must the chess player use his head, he must also take his fate into his own hands.

Nicolai Krogius, the Soviet grand master, psychologist and official, in his book *Psychology in Chess* maintains that the game is more than a grand; it is a brilliant means of education.

Perhaps Krogius loves chess and that is why he praises it so passionately, arguing that the game forces one to concentrate. It demands, mental clarity on the one hand and intuition on the other. It encourages independent thought because those who limit themselves to copying other masters and remain

In a chamber of the royal palace two aristocratic ladies of the court amuse themselves playing "the Game of Kings" as their attendants watch. (A miniature from the Alfonso the Wise *chess book.)*

passive otherwise will not get very far. The benefit of the mistakes that lead to self-assessment is also correctly praised. His argument becomes questionable when he discusses our time, a "period of scientific-technical revolution." Krogius thinks that the student of chess learns to find his way not only

on the board but also in the revolutionised world, where the work of the mind is more important than that of the body, and success depends on studying methods, not just mere facts. It is valid to take in a lot of information and to evaluate the really essential facts. It would be really nice to kill two birds of such different types — the perception of chess and the world — with one stone. But Krogius cannot name anybody who has done this in an exemplary way. Very wisely the Doctor of Psychology refrains from posing the obvious question as to whether a leading grand master, after a short period of retraining, would be capable of managing an industrial corporation, a party or an army. All that one can truly say is that for an intellectual person, chess is a more appropriate pastime than most other games. Who would say to a young beginner: "Study the structure of pawn chains and the peculiarities of castling so that you can make your way in life?" It would be far more sensible to say, "Occupy yourself with chess, you will enjoy it and it will enrich you, and it won't do you any harm to learn to concentrate and develop yourself."

Would that be good advice for a woman as well? Whenever chess is discussed, women are neglected in thought and word. When one hears something about two opponents, one imagines two men; when one is told something about a club, one pictures a male society. When someone sits down at the typewriter and

types the word "player," it is as if no woman player has come to his attention. Most women forgo, from the start, a pursuit in which they, because it is not a physical one, should actually be a good match for men, but in which they nevertheless are, for whatever reason, notoriously inferior. It is also true that a woman

has won the highest title, but she got it through competition with women. We have a World Champion in women's chess, who is no match for the World Champion who achieved his position competing among men. Until now, no single woman has played as well as Lasker or Capablanca, or Fischer or Kasparov.

When a woman has enough self-confidence to compete with men in grand master competition, she attracts attention. Vera Menchik was the first who dared to do this and sometimes won. There she sat with her round face and her big eyes, a character, an exception to the rule. In the twenties she was an almost unreal figure, but with her defeats she was, for the time being, proof that the glory of the men was not to be dimmed. Like Ms. Menchik subsequent women world champions also came from the Soviet Union. What they achieved seldom caught the eye and hardly ever appeared in a selection of top matches. Recently

A marriage contest. Hans Muelich painted this scene in 1552 showing Duke Albrecht V of Bavaria and his wife Anna of Austria playing against each other. They are being watched by the court and the citizenry. The miniature is taken from the Duchess's treasure book. It is preserved in the Bavarian State Library in Munich.

Three proven chess professionals and three females into the bargain — this has never heppened before. On the left, Zofia Polgar, born on November 2, 1974, in the middle Zsuzsa Polgar, born on April 19, 1969 and, on the right, Judit Polgar, born July 25, 1976 — and behind them the extremely proud parents.

Between the two World Wars, Vera Menchik was the great exception. Of Czech parentage, she had emigrated to London where she became the wife of an English chess organizer Rufus Stevenson. She played far better than any other woman in the world and regularly took part in men's tournaments.

Elizabeta Bykova was already a typical representative of women's chess and, with a two-year break, was World Champion from 1953—56 and 1958—62.

As was the case with other women, Olga Rubtsova, World Champion from 1956 until 1958, was completely overshadowed by men. Talk in the chess world at that time centered around Michail Botvinnik, Wassily Smyslov and other male champions.

Nona Gaprindaschwili was World Champion from 1962 to 1978. She once lost her temper: "Do you really think that a grand master shows a little bit of chivalry when playing against a woman? Not a hope." Men would be twice as afraid of losing when playing against a female opponent.

Maya Chiburdanidze has been World Champion since 1978. In the fall of 1988, she narrowly defended her title against Nana Joseliani.

a very young Hungarian, Zsuzsa Polgar, who laid claim to compete in the future with increasingly better men has attracted attention. No sooner had Zsuzsa pocketed her first triumphs than she introduced her sister into the world of chess, Judit, was still a child, but, as the adults were soon to discover, absolutely quick on the trigger. As a ten year-old, Judit beat seasoned amateurs, while presenting an image of excitement and ice coldness. Her body vibrated from her toes to her shoulders, but the looks that pierced through her narrowed eyes revealed a stable psyche and a heart of stone. Soon Judith gave the impression that one day she would terrify the men perhaps even more than Zsuzsa, and she has done so, having at the age of 12 achieved the title of international master. The middle sister, the beautiful Zofia, also recently stunned the international chess playing scene with some impressive victories. Regardless of how high the Polgars rise in the end the publicity they have been able to achieve for their sex is welcome. How sad it was, when the women used to sit and rack their brains in the same hall as the men during

Olympic chess championships and nobody except their coaches watched them, while at some of the male boards large crowds of people used to gather.

The game is often as colorful as the clothing and has just as little to do with international standards. The important thing for these ladies from Nigeria was to be there and they attended the 1988 Chess Olympics in Thessaloniki, attaining 49th place out of 56.

Opposite: *page 49 (verso) of the work* Livre des conquestes et faits d'Alexandre *by Jean Wauquelin. This is a work of about 250 pages of parchment manuscript ornamented with numerous miniatures. It originated in the second half of the 15th century and at one time belonged to the library of the Duke of Cleves. It was acquired in 1654 for the Ducal Library in Gotha.*

The parchment manuscript tells the story of Alexander the Great of Macedonia. The Sultan of Baudres, pictured on the left, was the nephew of the King of India who had laid siege to the city of Pheson. The inhabitants of this city captured the Sultan during one of their sorties and then treated him like a guest. He took part in court life and even played Chess with Princess Phesonne, seen here wearing the traditional costume of the Burgundian court of the 15th century! Alexander himself is not depicted; he and his troops were supporting the town in its battle.

THE NATIONAL SCHOOLS.

Delight in winning a game. An old Chinese playing chess on the streets of Peking.

Opposite: In Chinese chess, the "Elephant Game" (above the board the Chinese characters for Xiang Qi) the River Chu, as border to the land of the Han, divides the board into two kingdoms which are at war with each other. On the base line of each side there is a king's palace marked by two diagonals. The 16 pieces are placed where the lines cross, not on the squares. At start of play, the last row is composed of wagon, horse, general, minister, king, minister, general, horse, wagon; on the third line, there are two cannons and, on the fourth line, five soldiers.

At first glance the Chinese chess board is very similar to our chess board. It is a board with eight squares by nine, but the pieces do not stand on the squares — they stand on the intersections of the lines between them, which allows for nine men to be set up on the starting line. A "river," a wide band, also divides the playing area into two halves. In the elephant game, the river is the border between the countries of the Han and the Chu. White does not play against Black, but Red against Black. In European chess as well, the color red appears again and again, whether it be in the case of enameling pieces, or in the case of identification markings of white symbols on magnet or demonstration boards.

Han and Chu each have their own palace. Three pieces are not allowed to leave the palace: the king, who may only make a move forwards, backwards or to the side in each case, and his two advisors (ministers), who may only move diagonally. The freedom of movement of the general, two diagonal steps at a time, is limited to the land which he serves. The wagon, which is the equivalent of our castle or rook, may cross the river. The canon moves like the wagon, but can only take a piece by jumping over another piece. The horse's move is a leap as is our knight's move, but when another piece is standing next to it, its legs are hobbled in that direction. The soldier, our pawn, moves and captures forwards and after crossing the river, sideways

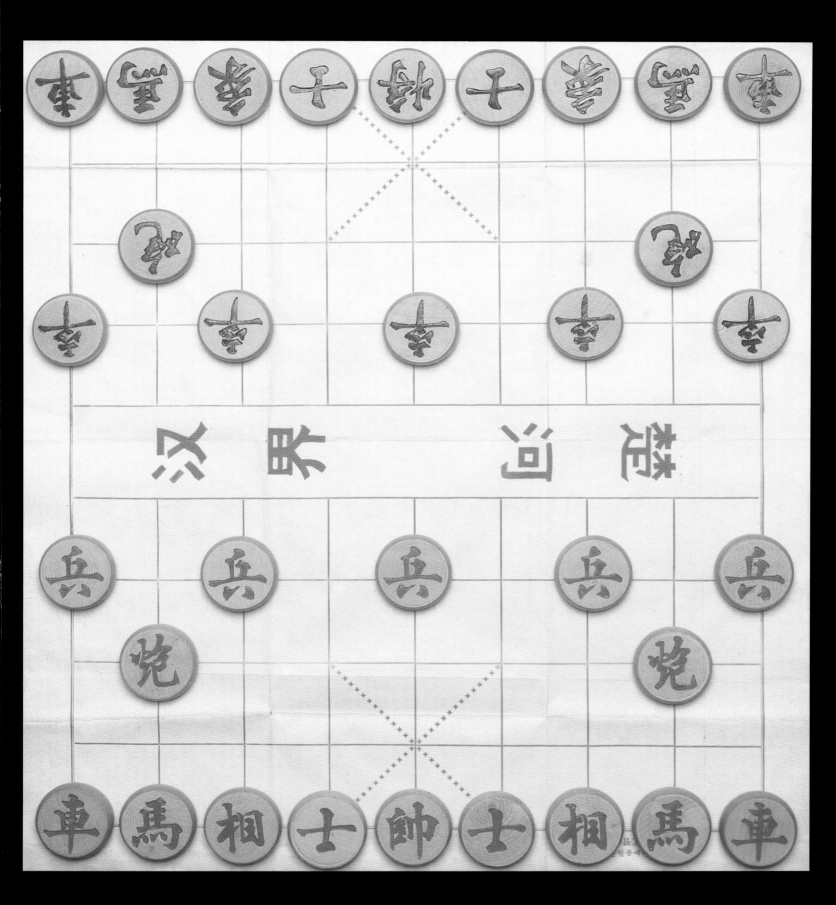

The Chinese have to be inventive in order to maintain their livelihood also in 1989. This Chinese is "selling" himself as a chess player. He is waiting patiently on the Yangtze bridge in Wuhan for an opponent.

There must always be one piece between the two kings; he is not allowed to move away to the side, because then the kings would be in mate.

To checkmate the opposing king is also the aim of the game as far as the Chinese are concerned. Stalemate is equivalent to mate, which is an advantage for the stronger side. On the other hand, a player who puts his opponent in mate three times in a row in the same position has not forced a draw but lost the game.

The captured piece vanishes from the board and is put down somewhere between the coffee cup, the notation slip and the ashtray. Instead of standing uselessly around, surely it could be put to use in the army of the one that captured it? That is the way the Japanese, whom the game also reached from India, see it. *Shogi,* Japanese chess, should not be mistaken for *Go.* While, in *Go,* the point of the game is, on a board with 361 intersections, to encircle the largest possible terrain and therefore to take possession of it, the aim of *Shogi,* as is that of Western chess, is to checkmate the king. But captured men can, immediately or later, be incorporated into one's own army. So one has black captured men in the white camp and vice versa? Therefore it is of advantage that both hosts differ from one another not in colour, but simply in the direction in which the pieces are facing. *Schogi* pieces are six millimeter-thick, painted and enamelled plywood platelets, with one side that is pointed and is in-

as well. A substitution on the opponent's base line is not possible. But where is the elephant, which gives the game its name? It is the black general, as opposed to the red general, which is called the chancellor. The kings also have different names: on the red side he is the commander-in-chief and on the black side he is called the commander.

Many Chinese chess-boards display the following message:
"Whoever moves his hand and does not draw back
is a great man.
The silent spectator is a true nobleman."

tended to be turned towards the enemy. Unlike the practice in Western chess, where only the pawn may be substituted, in Japan each piece, with the exception of the king and the golden general, has the prospect of being advanced. So, there must be a lot of material for exchange. Once again it is an advantage that the pieces are flat. One only has to turn the upper surface downwards and the lower surface upwards and the symbol for the new rank is immediately visible, which offers greater freedom of movement. The substitution is carried out not at the end of the board, but at an arbitrary point after entering the opposite camp, which takes up three rows, as the *Shogi* board has nine rows and

An opponent has been found! If the latter wins, he receives the simple game of chess in its blue box; if he loses, he has to pay for the game. The old man won this game in less than five minutes.

181

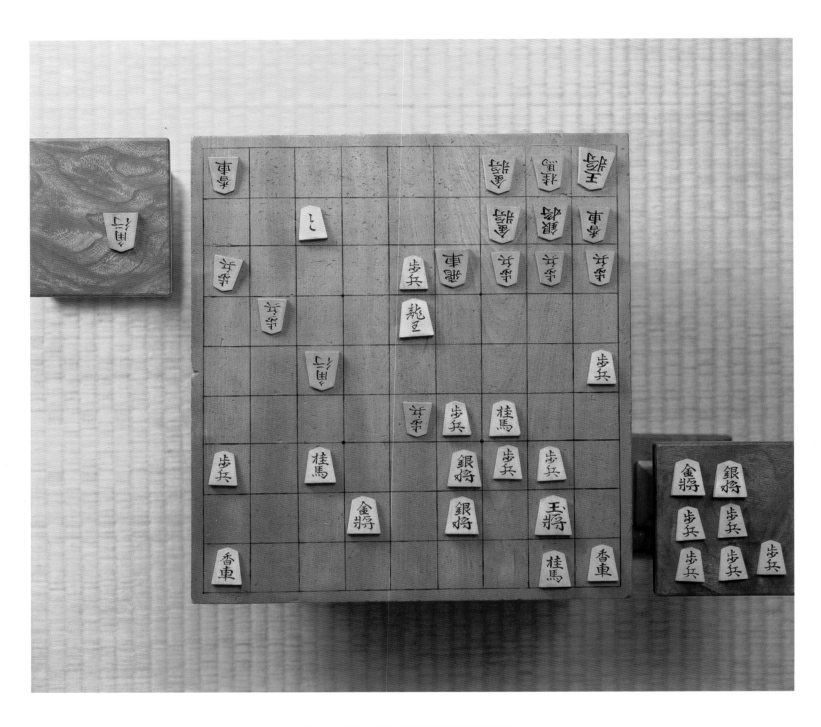

Above: *Positions in a game of Shogi, the Japanese version of chess, also known as the "Game of the Generals." Shogi reached Japan in the 8th century from Korea.*

Right: *Opening positions in Shogi. The board has 9 × 9 squares. The pieces are flat counters marked with Chinese characters.*

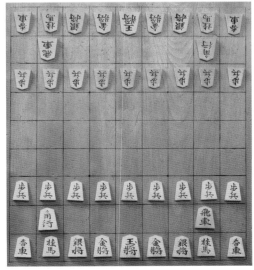

nine lines, which means there are a total of eighty-one fields. Pawns, lancers, knights and the silver general advance towards the golden general, the bishop towards the dragon, the rook towards the dragon king. In Japan the king, the rook and the bishop may move in the Western way. The qualities of the king and the bishop are unified in the dragon, those of the king and the rook in the dragon king. The pawn can only move and capture towards the front. What is least Western about the rest of the figures is not so much their different radius of action as the limitation of their freedom of movement to some of the total eight possible directions. Even the knight, who can jump as he does here, over other pieces too, may only do this forwards.

It is not totally wrong for the European chess lover to think with regard to nations too. For history teaches us that chess had its heyday in many countries then declined in popularity and fell into oblivion. The chess nation of the 16th century was Spain, the outstanding master Ruy Lopez, whose name is still used by the English for the Spanish opening. This cleric had the habit of looking for a good reason for each

move, thereby cultivating what was later to be somewhat arrogantly called "theory." In the 17th century, Italy swung the sceptre and produced sparkling tactical geniuses like Gioacchino Greco. Greco's sacrifice of White's king's bishop to break up the castled constellation for the purpose of preparing a mate attack using the queen and the king's knight, is still studied. But long before and long after 1800 nearly all leading masters were Frenchmen: Francois Philidor,

Japanese playing Go. Dyewood engraving by Utagawa Kuniyoshi from around 1900. This board game demands strategic insight and is not only popular in Japan. It originated in China where it is called Weiqi.

Below: The Shogi pieces are marked on both sides (provided that they can be converted), often with symbols: from left to right: king, rook, bishop, the golden general, the silver general, knight, lance-bearer and pawn.

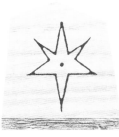

In my opinion, the most important gift which a great chess player must possess is a rich imagination. He must have the capacity to withdraw from a world of obtrusive realities into a domain of strange shapes and forms, which he combines to create new, unknown situations. Is this not what the composers of musical works do, to a certain extent? *Reuben Fine*

Alexandre Deschapelles, Louis Charles De La Bourdonnais, Pierre Saint-Amant. With Morphy and Staunton, an Anglo-American intermediate appeared, but in the second half of the 19th century chess became the domain of the Germans. It started with Adolf Anderssen and Louis Paulsen and did not quite end

Chess in New York's Washington Square Park. In the open air and surrounded by city bustle, Soviet emigré grand master Roman Dzindzichashvili will play brilliant, complicated chess against all comers, giving time or piece odds to make the bets fair. His dazzling style of play has an exhilarating effect on the public. He is the dark-haired, unshaven man in the crowd who is being watched by almost everybody.

with Siegbert Tarrasch and Emanuel Lasker. Wilhelm Steinitz, the first official World Champion, and Carl Schlechter brought honour to the Danube monarchy, as Vienna, around 1900, became the fortress of chess.

In the first half of our century, no country dominated international chess, and that was certainly a pleasant situation. This changed at one

stroke after the Second World War. Now the Soviet Union was *the* chess nation. The Soviets won the team world championships, the so-called Chess Olympics regularly. The game is extremely popular in the Soviet Union and is offered as an optional subject in schools. The likelihood of a talent remaining undiscovered is extremely slim. The grand masters are according to Western conception, civil servants. But it is far from the truth to say, as a sloppy use of language suggests, that there is a Russian behind every Soviet master: Botvinnik, a Jew; Bronstein, one of his challengers, a Jew; Tal, a Jew; Jefim Geller, a star of the sixties, a Ukrainian; Petrosyan, an Armenian; Keres, an Estonian; finally Kasparov, on the paternal side a Jew, on the maternal side an Armenian.

Among the Slavs, it was also the Yugoslavs who attracted attention as the reservoir of the highly talented in the years after 1945. In 1980 the country had 27 grand masters. The magazine *Chess Informer* which has appeared biannually since 1966, is one of the most important international chess magazines. Of equal importance is the *Encyclopedia of Chess Openings,* which appeared in five volumes between 1976 and 1980.

For many years a man of small stature sat at the master board, Svetozar Gligorić, a smooth customer when it came to position playing, a master of the closed position, and a threat to everyone, including rising and past world champions of the Soviet Union. Between 1947

and 1965, he won the Yugoslavian championship 11 times. He played for Yugoslavia in all the Olympics between 1950 and 1978. Gligorić found his match among the Hungarian grand masters in Lajos Portisch. Both had complete command and knew the ins and outs of their trade, belonged to the international elite, were told by their flatterers that they had it in them to win the

highest title, and were only occasionally able to rouse themselves to brilliant combinations. However, both of them inspired many players in their countries of origin to emulate them. The fame of Euwe, the World Champion, has had a similar effect in the Netherlands since the 1930s. Before Euve became World Champion in his match against Alekhine in 1935, the Royal

Absolute tranquillity. Warm evening, pleasant company, no high-level tension and each of the players is intent on whiling away the time. This idyll was photographed in 1989 in Zurich. It depicts the layman's expertise which is more forgiving than that of a master's ambition. Eventually, one of the men will stand up leisurely to move a piece or a pawn to another square — under the critical but kindly gaze of the bystanders.

Horses of flesh and blood are an even greater attraction in "Live Chess" than people of flesh and blood. Tactically, the use of a knight might be out of order — but loved by the public, since the horse gets to move.

Netherlands Chess League, which was founded in 1873, did not have more than 4,000 players. After his victory, the number rose to 11,000 members and in 1940 there were already 17,000. Compare this development with that of neighboring Belgium. A look at the newspapers tells us that in the south of both countries interest in chess is average, but in the north, on the other hand, the interest in local and foreign grand masters meets with extraordinarily lively response. As in Yugoslavia, many well-manned competitions were held, in the Netherlands where sponsors with substantial means gave the game a big lift. The Dutch national hope was and is Jan Timman. Timman came very close to the top with his game, which is lively, appealing to the public and rich in combinations, but he has to date failed to make the grade several times.

The questions as to whether someone is overwhelmingly good or just very good has tormented and fascinated friends of chess since the start of the game. Recently, this question has been raised by the successes of some English players. Since Staunton, continental chess players have crossed the British Channel, if at all, at Christmas, when a traditional competition was held in Hastings. Apart from this occasion, the British Isles did not appear to offer fertile terrain for the passion of chess. This impression was destroyed at one stroke in the eighties. Suddenly to the amazement of Europe, three masterminds arose: John Nunn, Jonathan Speel-

man and Nigel Short. The English attract attention to chess with their consistently sound, generally very detailed and amusing literature on the subject. Iceland has produced a few grand masters recently. Naturally, the Icelandic nights, which in winter hardly give way to day but to a kind of dawn light, are ideal for the pursuit of an intellectual game. But Iceland's severe climate with its short ration of sunlight, has not brought forth a single important chess player, so one cannot attribute the chess boom to it. The initial spark was rather the historic occasion of the World Championship Match between Fischer and Spassky, in Reykjavik, 1972.

By 1970 everyone had come to terms with the fact that within a reasonable space of time only the Soviet Union would produce World Champions. This is the background against which one has to see the rise of Robert Fischer, who made it his business to upset Russia's hegemony. The whole world, Bobby included, saw it like this: A western loner challenged an empire. According to the rules of the World Chess Federation (FIDE) everyone who wanted to try for the top title had to go through three candidate competitions before he had the right to sit down at a table with the World Champion, who was then Boris Spassky. The first candidate who faced the American Fischer was the Soviet player Taimanov, who was not an exceptional, but still a fairly good, grand master and who was especially skilled in the theory of openings. Taimanov was sensation-

ally beaten — he lost 0:6. Nobody could remember another candidate's match with a hundred percent result. On his return home, not having managed to gain even a single draw, Taimanov's life was no longer a bed of roses.

Now the Soviet's hope was pinned on a foreigner, on Bent Larsen, the "lion" from Denmark. In the West he was also held to be, if not better, at least more experienced than Fischer. Then something incomprehensible happened:

the impossible happened again. Larsen also lost 0:6. Apart from the fact that the dangerous Dane was only a shadow of himself after this horrible experience, Moscow functionaries realised that Fischer was to be feared. The third candidate to go on his way was the heavyweight, Tigran Petrosyan. In his autobiography, Viktor Korchnoi quotes the opinion of Botvinnik, "that Petrosyan is a rare exception. He is no creative spirit, but is a destroyer of existing values." Korchnoi adds: "One is almost tempted to show re-

"Live Chess" on the Grande Place in Brussels, one of the most beautiful squares in the world. In 1988, members of a theater group followed the directions of a historically costumed announcer, who, for her part, was only relaying via microphone what grand masters Timman and Karpov were pondering at an unseen table. The game lasted a good hour and ended in a draw. The square had been the setting for more gruesome events. More than four hundred years previously, approximately on the site where Timman and Karpov were pondering, two heroes of the Dutch resistance against the Spanish, the Dukes of Egmont and Hoorne, were executed.

A rather unusual public was in attendance at the opening ceremony of the Chess Olympics in 1986. The team World Championships for men and women were taking place in Dubai. The United Arab Emirates are everything but chess oases, they are part of the Third World, to which the President of the World Chess Association, Florencio Campomanes, who originates from the Philippines, pays a great deal of attention.

spect for the devilish willpower and the inventiveness of this man." It was now up to Petrosyan to stop the American. Strangely enough the people believed him, the ex-World Champion, to be more capable of defeating Fischer than Spassky, the defender of the title. Indeed, Petrosyan was the world's best brakeman. For a moment it looked as if it would work out for the Soviets, because, after five games they were equal. But then the brake failed, and Fischer continued on his triumphant trail.

Before the deciding game in Reykjavik in 1972, the American was regarded as the favorite. But suddenly he stood in his own way. He failed to leave for Iceland on time, so that the world championship match had to be postponed for a few days. He spoiled his first game with a surprising bishop sacrifice, which is seen, according to one's discretion, as a crude mistake, as a preliminary to a subtle, but shaky combination, or as an attempt to cause complications. Fischer did not appear at all for the second game. Now the match was 0:2 for Spassky. Fischer succeeded in having the third game played, not like the first one, on a stage in a hall, but in an adjoining room. Spassky opened with White 1 d4. But Fischer did not answer. He sat there, pale as death. At that moment, it looked as if the competition would break down. Fischer was a person who, with grim exclusivity, had only lived for chess, who had only one goal before his eyes, the World Championship. Psychologists know this frantic fear before the final step. After five minutes, a painfully long span of time for those who were there, Fischer's fingers reached for the king's knight and moved it to f6. The spell was broken. In the deep and difficult game that followed, Bobby achieved one of his greatest feats. After 21 competitive games, he had managed to triumph over Spassky, no, over a great power. In newspapers every world championship has been labeled "The Fight of the Century." But this honor has only been deserved by two encounters: Alekhine – Capablanca, 1927 and Fischer – Spassky, 1972. Fischer is responsible for interest in chess making a dramatic jump throughout the world.

"In one game which I played against him several years ago, he lost a pawn without any compensation. Then he played on as if the loss of a pawn was trivial. While I was trying to work out what he was up to, I made a mistake and lost the game. Spassky has the same expressionless look when at the board both when he checkmates his opponent or is himself checkmated. He can mess up a piece and you are never completely sure whether it's a mistake or an unbelievably profound sacrifice."

*Bobby Fischer
on a game lost to Spassky*

Because Bobby withdrew from chess after having achieved the World Championship and did not defend the title in 1975 according to the rules, it passed on to Anatoly Karpov without a competition, by bureaucratic decision. The next two World Championships also took on a political coloring. Karpov, a true Russian and true son of the "working-class" and therefore a World Champion who was absolutely to the taste of the Moscow functionaries, did not in 1978 and 1981 have to face an American, but instead a Russian emigrant, Victor Korchnoi, the deserving senior citizen, who was suddenly denounced as a traitor to his fatherland. The age difference of 20 years was certainly an ad-

vantage to Korchnoi. Nevertheless, the younger Karpov won the first match by the skin of his teeth and the second match without any trouble.

In 1984 the true rival for Karpov appeared in the form of Garry Kasparov. Ka. and Ka.: these are the great warring chess giants of our time. Their duels went on and on thanks to the biased ruling of the Philippino President of the World Chess Federation, Florencio Campomanes, who was blatantly on Karpov's side. Kasparov took to referring to his opponent as "Karpomanes." Within four years there were four World Championship matches, which was a record. The first contest should have been decided

At almost all the big contests in the 60's, 70's and 80's, one onlooker appeared who aroused admiration and amazement: the grand master Miguel Najdorf, who was born in Poland in 1910 and was currently living in Argentina. Admiration because he was a brilliant tactician and one of the best blindfold players; amazement because his knowledge of chess was still at its best. When analysis was being carried out on the fringes of the 1987 World Championship in Seville, he understood immediately what was being shown to him by a far younger man, Boris Spassky. Spassky was defeated by Fischer in 1972 in Reykjavik, an event that had been foreseen by Najdorf. He had always considered the American to be the superior player.

"When the chess world wants to enjoy the pleasure, excitement and instruction that a world championship offers to several hundred thousand chess players even, to a certain extent, to future generations, why should they not pay for it? Why does the chess world expect all sacrifices to be made by the masters, why can't an organization be set up if the whole question revolves around a really paltry sum of money?"

Emanuel Lasker

Right: *Putting a strain on the brain (almost) anywhere, even just above water level. A linoleum chess-board can be laid on almost all surfaces, so long as this is more or less stable. Budapest has a lot of thermal baths with chess facilities. None of the more mature gentlemen here played as well as the girl with the spaghetti straps, the then 16-year-old Zsuzsa Polgar.*

after six matches had been won by one of the parties, but this did not happen, instead Campomanes broke it off after 48 games, ostensibly because the match had lasted too long, but in fact, it was because Kasparov had managed to cut down his deficit from 1:5 to 3:5 in the last two games. Kasparov won the title in the second match, which was limited to 24 games, and narrowly defended it in the third and even more narrowly in the fourth. The insignificance of this gap, which was flattering to the loser, already leads one to doubt the thesis of Kasparov's book *Political Game,* which amazed chess lovers who were not into metaphysical thinking. Kasparov writes that his games against Karpov have more significance than mere games against another chess master, they were supposed to symbolize the conflict between the two opposing political principles represented by Gorbachev and Brezhnev for the fight of good against evil.

To compare a chess match to world politics is ridiculous, like a wild combination without a sufficient positional basis. In any case, the two top players of the Soviet Union face each other with an aversion, which could not be stronger if they represented different nations. But the last word has not been spoken and their last game has not been played.

190

> "Even for the best masters, a contest for the crown will be an exceptional situation. Correspondingly, tension runs incomparably high. In addition, there are other events which have an incalculable psychological effect."
>
> *Garry Kasparov*

THE MASTERS AND THEIR GAMES

Garry Kasparov playing during the World Championship against Anatoly Karpov in Seville in December 1987.

Opposite: *The knight, approximately the same in value as a bishop; in endgames, however, the knight is superior due to its greater mobility.*
Russian work, bone, 18th century.

Everyone recognizes beauty. But everyone has trouble defining it. With beautiful games, it is the same. Many prizes for beauty have already been awarded; numerous anthologies about the most beautiful, or the most brilliant or the most exciting games have been published. But each selection contains a subjective element, which does not mean, however, that everything is merely a question of taste. All agree on certain things. Nobody would call a match that is full of mistakes or one marked by uncertainty on both sides beautiful, nor would anybody think of giving special praise to a series of correct but average moves. Aesthetics come to bear only on games where exceptional quality is obvious.

The selection of the games in this chapter has been made for the reader, who wants to experience the aesthetics of chess. An addition, the thoughts of the grand masters should give great pleasure. The high quality of the examples offered is beyond doubt, and with them enjoyment of the game should be awakened. That is why games with brilliant combinations have been given preference. The study of heavy positioned games in which the finest nuances are important from beginning to end, is a must for the prospective professional, but superfluous for the enthusiastic amateur. Length was a criterion in the selection, too. Those who want to enjoy a whole match, and not just this or that detail, must see it as a whole, which creates a considerable

The queen.

The king.

The chess figures of Gustavus Selenus in Chess or the Game of Kings, *Leipzig, 1616.*

problem after the 40th or 50th move. Luckily the treasury of chess offers some brilliant and clear examples.

THE IMMORTAL

(London 1851)
White: Adolph Anderssen
Black: Lionel Kieseritzky

The grammar school teacher from Breslau won the "Immortal Game" against one of his strongest contemporaries. Why did this game, curiously enough not played in the famous London tournament, which was won by Anderssen but which was played afterwards, become the "Immortal"? Because it incorporated the ideals of beauty. The way in which Anderssen attacked, the way he exposed his king, the way he sacrificed his bishop and then immediately both castles and finally even the queen — this series of foolhardy actions is the epitome of chess. Such a reckless style of play has a touch of mortality through and through. This game deserves true immortality also because of the incredible risks taken, but more so because of the fantastic economy of means with which the moves are executed. It was a triumph of tactical, but even more so of strategic, ability.

1.e4 e5 2.f4 (King's Gambit) ef4: 3.Bc4 Qh4+ 4.Kf1 b5 (a whim of Kieseritzky) 5.Bb5: Ktf6 6.Ktf3 Qh6 7.d3 Kth5 8.Kth4 Qg5 9.Ktf5 c6 10.Rg1 cb5: 11.g4 Ktf6 12.h4 Qg6 13.h5 Qg5 14.Qf3 Ktg8 (otherwise the Queen would be lost) 15.Bf4: Qf6 16.Ktc3 Bc5 17.Ktd5 Qb2: (see diagram)

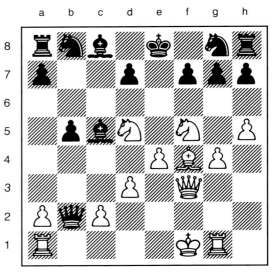

18.Bd6 Qa1:+ 19.Ke2 Bg1: 20.e5 (blocks the diagonal) Kta6 21. Ktg7:+ Kd8 22.Qf6+ Ktf6: 23.Be7 mate.

ACCORDING TO MUSIC OF ROSSINI

(Paris 1858)
White: Paul Morphy
Black: Duke of Braunschweig and Count Isouard

While Rossini's *Barber of Seville* was being performed on stage, Morphy created a second masterpiece in a box at the Paris Opera. Some authors have found fault with this, the most popular of his quick wins, saying that the opposing duo was too weak, which made the victory too easy. Well, in competition with top class masterminds, many players have already cut a somewhat poor figure, not only this Count and this Duke. Apart from that the two aristocrats were of a quality that is normal for amateurs; that is why the short work that Morphy made of it should be worth looking at and of instructive value for all. On the other hand, only a game of such high quality can excuse the fact that the guest from the United States did not give his undivided attention to the delightful music.

1.e4 e5 2.Ktf3 d6 (Philidor defence) 3.d4 Bg4 4.de5: Bf3: 5.Qf3: de5: 6.Bc4 Ktf6 7.Qb3 Qe7 8.Ktc3 c6 9.Bg5 b5 (the decisive mistake) 10. Ktb5: cb5: 11.Bb5:+ Ktbd7 12.0-0-0 Rd8 13.Rd7: (so that the containment remains) Rd7: 14.Rd1 Qe6 15.Bd7: + Ktd7: (see diagram)

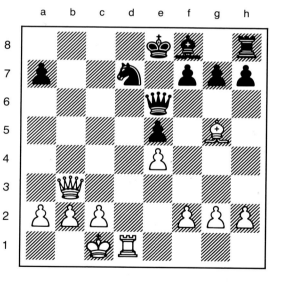

16.Qb8 + Ktb8: 17.Rd8 mate.

THE MOST BEAUTIFUL MOVE

(Breslau 1912)
White: Stepan Lewitzki
Black: Frank Marshall

The game Lewitzki – Marshall was just good up to the 23rd move of White. But now (see diagram)

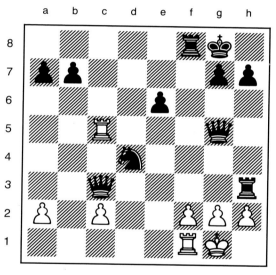

a bolt came out of the blue, the legendary move 23. ... Qg3, which Marshall called the most beautiful of his life. It is the most beautiful of all! The queen exposed herself to fire from three sides. The spectators could not believe their eyes; those who were following the play thought there had been a printing error. The move is bold and well thought out. Threatens 24. ... Qh2: mate. The joke is that 24.hg3: will fail because 24. ... Kte2 mates and 24.fg3: will also fail because 24. ... Kte2+ 25.Kh1 Rf1: mate. For better or worse, Lewitzki decided in favor of 24.Qg3: Kte2 +

The rook (castle).

A soldier (pawn).

A messenger (knight).

25.Kh1 Ktg3: + 26.Kg1 Ktf1: 27.gh3: Ktd2. (As Black held most of the pieces, White gave up.)

ALL VERY EASY

(St. Petersburg 1914)
White: Ossip Bernstein
Black: José Raúl Capablanca

Capablanca was particularly proud of this win because his method of working with the simplest of means functioned with rare smoothness and led to one of the most wonderful sensations in chess history. The game is an outstanding object lesson for amateurs, especially because of its simplicity. But was the backward and forward movement of the rook on the c line just childish? It was only intended to appear so. In reality, Capablanca had the final combination unshakably before his eyes. Not even this is affected. It is elemental.

1.d4 d5 2.c4 e6 3.Ktc3 Ktf6 (refused queen's gambit) 4.Ktf3 Be7 5.Bg5 0-0 6.e3 Ktbd7 7.Rc1 b6 8.cd5: ed5: 9.Qa4 Bb7 10.Ba6 Ba6: 11.Qa6: c5 12.Bf6: Ktf6: 13.dc5: bc5: 14.0-0 Qb6 15.Qe2 (the substitution of the queen would have improved Black's position) c4 16.Rfd1 Rfd8 17.Ktd4 Bb4 18.b3 Rac8 19.bc4: dc4: 20.Rc2 (aims at doubling the rook) Bc3: 21.Rc3: Ktd5 22.Rc2 c3 23.Rdc1 Rc5 (the trap …) 24.Ktb3 Rc6 25.Ktd4 Rc7 26.Ktb5 Rc5 27.Ktc3: (… has shut) Ktc3: 28.Rc3: Rc3: 29.Rc3: (see diagram). Did Bernstein hope for 29. … Qb1 + 30.Qf1 Rd1 31.Rc8 + ? Capablanca moved 29. … Qb2. That meant mate or winning the rook. White therefore conceded.

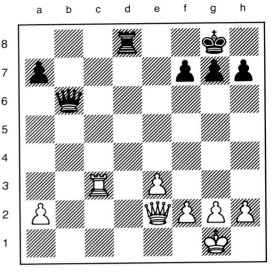

HIGHLIGHT OF THE AMATEUR

(New Orleans 1921)
White: Adams
Black: Torre

It is probable that the amateur finds the time spent on master games of little advantage. He yearns to play such brilliant moves, but shouldn't he know his limits? When he feels discouraged, there is only one thing to do — look to a certain Adams, who was a nobody and achieved an overwhelmingly beautiful combination against Señor Torre. It looks like a combination that has been carefully constructed by highly skilled professionals. But no, it was conjured up effortlessly by the hand of an amateur. Amateurs, keep the unknown Mr. Adams constantly in mind!

1.e4 e5 2.Ktf3 d6 (Philidor defence) 3.d4 ed4: 4.Qd4: Ktc6 5.Bb5 Bd7 6.Bc6: Bc6: 7.Ktc3 Ktf6 8.0-0 Be7 9.Ktd5 Bd5: 10.ed5: 0-0 11.Bg5 c6 12.c4 cd5: 13.cd5: Re8 14.Rfe1 a5

15.Re2 Rc8 16.Rael Qd7 17.Bf6: Bf6: (see diagram). Until this point it was

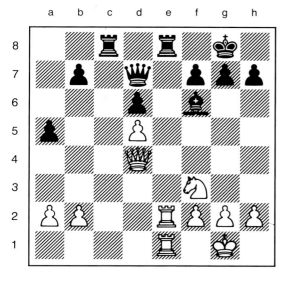

the everyday work of mortals. But now it was as if Apollo approached the board. 18.Qg4 (the queen is taboo and will remain so till the end) Qb5 19.Qc4 Qd7 20.Qc7 Qb5 21.a4 Qa4: 22.Re4 Qb5 23.Qb7: Black conceded, because 23. … Rb8 24.Qb5: would have been hopeless. The dream had become reality.

EXTREMELY COMPLICATED

(Baden-Baden 1925)
White: Richard Réti
Black: Alexander Alekhine

Alekhine had bad luck as far as prizes for refinement were concerned. If he played particularly brilliantly according to his lights, he didn't get a prize because there were none. This is also how it was in this case. "The position is extremely complicated and full of beautiful combinations," was his comment on his 27th move. That was the

highest self-congratulation that he could allow himself to write. Réti fought wonderfully, but Alekhine was slightly better. Only in the last move was the game decided.

1.g3 (king's fianchetto) e5 2.Ktf3 e4 3.Ktd4 d5 4.d3 ed3: 5.Qd3: Ktf6 6.Bg2 Bb4+ 7.Bd2 Bd2:+ 8.Ktd2: 0-0 9.c4 Kta6 10.cd5: Ktb4 11.Qc4 Ktbd5: 12.Kt2b3 c6 13.0-0 Re8 14.Rfd1 Bg4 15.Rd2 Qc8 16.Ktc5 Bh3 17.Bf3 Bg4 18.Bg2 Bh3 19.Bf3 Bg4 20. Bh1 h5 21.b4 a6 22.Rc1 h4 23.a4 hg3: 24.hg3: Qc7 25.b5 ab5: 26.ab5: (see diagram)

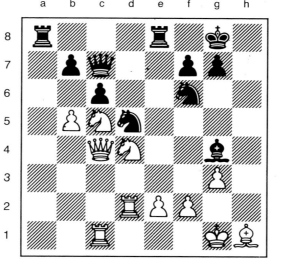

26. … Re3 27.Ktf3 cb5: 28.Qb5: Ktc3 29.Qb7: Qb7: 30.Ktb7: Kte2:+ 31.Kh2 Kte4 32. Rc4 Ktf2: 33.Bg2 Be6 34.Rc2 Ktg4+ 35.Kh3 Kte5+ 36.Kh2 Rf3: 37.Re2: Ktg4+ 28.Kh3 Kte3+ 39.Kh2 Ktc2: 40.Bf3: Ktd4. White conceded because of 41.Re3 Ktf3:+ 42.Rf3: Bd5.

Such a game deserves variations:

a) 27.fe3: Qg3:+

b) 27.Kh2 Ra3 28.Ktcb3 Qe5 29.bc6: bc6: 30.fe3: Qh5+ 31Kg1 Qh3

c) 27.Bf3 Bf3: 28.ef3: cb5: 29.Ktb5: Qa5 30.Rd5: Re1+ 31Re1: Qe1:+ 32.Kg2 Ra1

The man (bishop).

The intriguer (jester, bishop).

d) 31.Kf1 Ktg3: + 32.fg3: Bf3:
33.Bf3: Rf3: + 34.Kg2 R8a3 35.Rd8 +
Kh7 36.Rh1 + Kg6 37.Rh3 Rfb3

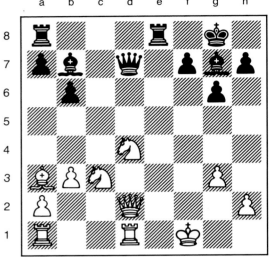

BLACK WINS
As quickly as possible

(New York 1964)
White: Robert Byrne
Black: Robert Fischer

This game is a miracle. Because normally someone who gives up after 21 moves has made a huge mistake. This loss must have been especially trenchant if the loser was even playing White. But in this case White was not guilty of such a mistake. It was no more than an inaccuracy, to move the king's rook in the 14th move, and not the queen's rook, which would have been better. How could White imagine what was to follow? Basically one can only accuse Byrne of being less inventive and brilliant than Fischer.

1.d4 Ktf6 2.c4 g6 3.g3 c6 4.Bg2 d5 (Grünfeld defence) 5.cd5: cd5: 6.Ktc3 Bg7 7.e3 0-0 8.Ktge2 Ktc6 9.0-0 b6 10.b3 Ba6 11.Ba3 Re8 12.Qd2 e5 13.de5: Kte5: 14.Rfd1 Ktd3 15.Qc2 (because of the threat 15. ... Kte4) Ktf2: 16.Kf2: Ktg4 + 17.Kg1 Kte3: 18.Qd2 Ktg2: (for once the bishop is more valuable than the rook) 19.Kg2: d4 20.Ktd4: Bb7 + 21.Kf1 Qd7 (see diagram)

White conceded, which the winner later called a "bitter disappointment." Fischer would have enjoyed seeing 22.Qf2 Qh3 + 23.Kg1 Re1 + 24.Re1: Bd4: on the board, or for that matter 22.Kt db5 Qh3 + 23.Kg1 Bh6.

BLACK WINS
Even faster

(Belgrade 1970)
White: Bent Larsen
Black: Boris Spassky

This game is even shorter and was also won by Black, but with Bent Larsen, unlike Robert Byrne, the mistakes are clear. The build-up of White was meant to be modern, but it turned out to be clumsy. For one thing, Larsen neglected his right wing. That would not have been worth mentioning at all if Spassky, who happened to be World Champion at the time, had not laid his opponent's mistakes bare with such breathtaking relentlessness. Robust impartiality was always a sign of the quality of this practitioner, but even a very good player achieves such an incendiary effect only once in his life.

1.b3 e5 2.Bb2 Ktc6 (erratic; some also call it (Larsen opening) 3.c4 Ktf6 4.Ktf3 e4 5.Ktd4 Bc5 6.Ktc6: dc6: 7.e3 Bf5 8.Qc2 Qe7 9.Be2 0-0-0 10.f4 (now the cup was filled to the brim)

A marksman (knight).

198

Ktg4 11.g3 h5 12.h3 h4 13. (Larsen thought for 1 hour) hg4: hg3: 14. Rg1

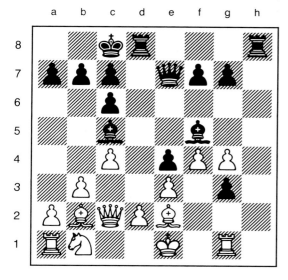

14. ... Rh1 (the bomb – from this moment on White was lost in every variation) 15.Rh1: g2 16.Rf1 (16.Rg1 was of no use because 16. ... Qh4+ besides Qh1) Qh4+ 17.Kd1 gf1: Q+. White conceded.

The game derives from a competition of the Soviet Union against the (officially named) rest of the world that was staged on 10 boards and one that the rest of the world lost by a narrow margin.

THE SECRET OF THE SWING

(Nikšić 1983)
White: Garry Kasparov
Black: Lajos Portisch

Fantasy, dynamism, temperament — by the age of 20, Kasparov had developed his individual style to perfection. The circumspect Lajos Portisch, 26 years older, who had been Hungary's best player for one generation, was exactly the right man to test the solidity of Kasparov's style.

1.d4 Ktf6 2.c4 e6 3.Ktf3 b6 4.Ktc3 Bb7 (Queen's Indian) 5.a3 d5 6.cd5: Ktd5: 7.e3 Ktc3: 8.bc3: Be7 9.Bb5+ c6 10.Bd3 c5 11.0-0 Ktc6 12.Bb2 Rc8 13. Qe2 0-0 14.Rad1 Qc7 15.c4 cd4: 16.ed4: Kta5 17.d5 ed5: 18.cd5: Bd5: 19.Bh7: + Kh7: 20.Rd5: Kg8 (see diagram)

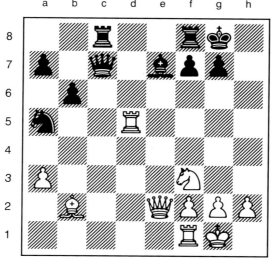

21.Bg7: Kg7: 22.Kte5 Rfd8 (covers the square d7) 23.Qg4+ Kf8 24.Qf5 f6 25.Ktd7+ Rd7: 26.Rd7: Qc5 27.Qh7 Rc7 28.Qh8+ (bypasses a trap) Kf7 29.Rd3 Ktc4 30.Rfd1 Kte5 (according to Kasparov a mistake, 30. ... Bd6 would be better) 31.Qh7+ Ke6 32. Qg8+ Kf5 33.g4+ Kf4 34.Rd4+ Kf3 35.Qb3+. Black conceded.

Kasparov sacrificed one piece in the position shown on the diagram. He was in the position to be this bold without the guarantee of an immediate mate offer only because his opponent was in reality playing with one piece less. The black rook remained inactive. This great game teaches two things: 1) all, not only most of the pieces, have to be active; and 2) every move should affect the whole board.

A rider (castle).

199

THE GREAT MASTERS

Top-class chess is not simply a do-or-die attack. Even a firebrand like Kasparov occasionally attempts to overcome his opponent by strategic measures. A contest of this type — tough, calm and 50 moves in length — was the 8th game at the World Championships held in Seville in 1987, in which Kasparov, white, beat his challenger Karpov. Botvinnik, Smyslov and Speelman considered this the best game of the match.

ALEXANDER ALEKHINE, who was born in Moscow in 1892 and died in Lisbon in 1946, was World Champion from 1927 to 1935 and from 1937 till his death. His game was characterised by unique dynamism. Alekhine always tried to keep the initiative for himself, to control the rules for dealing. His talent for revitalising "dead" draw situations and turning them into winning positions became legendary. The goal orientation that marked Alekhine's very complicated game saved it from becoming extravagant or ludicrous. When Alekhine set his sights on the World Championship, he was seen as a virtuoso player and a brilliant author — his books on the New York International Tournament games of 1924 and 1927 are classics — but not as a serious adversary for the World Champion Capablanca. To the amazement of the chess world, Alekhine won the 1927 match in Buenos Aires by 6:3 with 25 draws because he attacked the Cuban with his own weapon, a solid positional style. This was the beginning of Alekhine's prime time.

In the tournaments that followed he did not lose one game: Bradley Beach 1929, San Remo 1930, Bled 1931, London 1932, Paris 1933, Hastings 1934. But he was still afraid of Capablanca and denied him the return game, preferring to play the title fights against the obviously weaker Efim Bogoljubov in 1929 and 1934. The sensation occurred in 1935, when Alekhine lost the title 8:9 with 13 draws to the Dutchman, Max Euwe, whom he had completely underestimated. Alekhine had always been very critical of himself; he changed his life style and his drinking habits. In 1937, in various cities in the Netherlands he took the title from Euwe without any trouble, 10:4 with 11 draws. From now on, however, his game became obviously weaker. The fact that Alekhine performed mainly in the territories controlled by the National Socialists was not forgiven him right up until his death. The great player, who left his homeland after the October Revolution, died lonely, poor and ostracized in Portugal. He heard about the challenge of the young Botvinnik before he died. Whether Alekhine would have had a chance against such a player is more than questionable.

ADOLF ANDERSSEN was born in Breslau in 1818 and died there in 1879. With his inventiveness and his stupendous combinative power, this brilliant player, the greatest Germany has ever produced, was considered the greatest player in the world for many years. His artistry was only overshadowed by that of Paul Morphy for a little while. Anderssen is the creator of the "Immortal Game" (London 1851) and the "Evergreen Game" (Berlin 1853) — these are expressions that prove how greatly he fascinated the public. In 1851 Anderssen won the first big modern tournament in London but was nevertheless defeated by the still more brilliant Morphy in the Paris match in 1858. Anderssen taught mathematics at a Breslau grammar school and therefore did not have much time to go on chess trips, but nevertheless measured himself against the greats of his time. In this way he managed to beat two important masters, Johann Zukertort and Louis Paulsen. In 1866 he lost to Steinitz, who because of this unofficially called himself the World Champion. It was a symbolic defeat: the combinative artist defeated by the father of the positional game. Six wins, eight losses and not one draw! No really good master today manages what Anderssen knew and could achieve. But still the realm of the mind, which the teacher from Breslau commanded, seems to us like a lost paradise.

MICHAIL BOTVINNIK, who was born in 1911 in St. Petersburg, was World Champion from 1948 to 1963 with two short breaks. These interruptions throw light on his method of working; when he lost the world championship match in 1957 to Smyslov as in 1960 to Tal, he studied the peculiarities and weaknesses of his adversary so precisely, that in both cases he regained the lost title in the following year. Botvinnik always worked himself hard. His life style was almost ascetic, especially before important meets. A trained electrical engineer, he regarded steely self-discipline and a full study of all phases of chess play, as well as his opponents' styles, as basic requirements for success. Botvinnik's great tournament achievement came in 1935 when he shared the first place with Salo Flohr in Moscow, and in 1936 again a shared first place with Capablanca in Nottingham.

After the war Botvinnik won the Groningen Tournament (1946) and the Moscow Tournament (1947). He won the 1948 World Championship, which was played out in the Hague and in Moscow as a tournament of five, against Vasiliyevich Smyslov, Paul Keres, Samuel Reshevsky and Max Euwe. In later title matches he held his ground against Bronstein (1951) and Smyslov (1954). In 1963, at the age of 52, he finally handed over the title of World Champion to Tigran Petrosyan. Botvinnik's game are technically perfect, but they lack brilliance. The lover of science tried to put an end to the "playful"

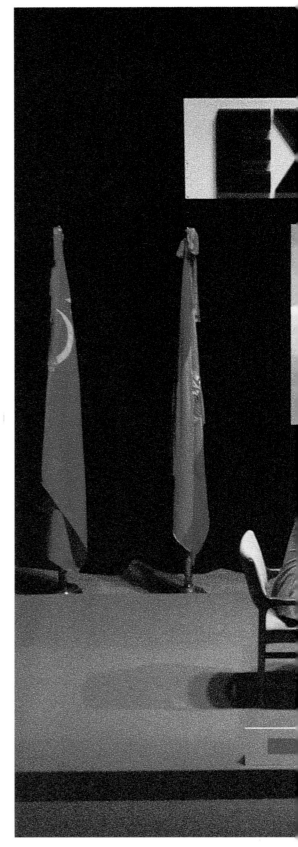

> "The study of chess history is important, a thorough familiarity with the creations of grand masters of the past, profound knowledge of the development of different tendencies and ideas in chess, which is also a basic requirement for one's own future successes."
>
> *Michail Botvinnik*

chess style. He was, like Alekhine, an unmerciful critic of himself and had a sure eye for young talent. Botvinnik was the first in the Soviet Union to notice Fischer's outstanding talent and to officially point it out.

JOSÉ RAÚL CAPABLANCA Y GRAUPERA, was born in Havana in 1888 and died in New York in 1942. He was World Champion from 1921–1927. Capablanca was unsurpassed in the art of grasping at a glance the secrets of a position, its weaknesses and its strengths. He aimed at simple solutions and avoided all complexity. He developed in a goaloriented way without ever hurrying things, positive aspects of a position even if they were minimal. His nickname was Chess Machine. Robert Fischer once said that for him each Capablanca move was immediately understandable. Capablanca's game appeared to be effortless, a misconception based upon his prodigious beginnings, by his opinion that chess has been researched and will die a "stalemate death" within a short time, as well as by his elegant, man-of-the-world appearance. Lasker looked deeper: "Probably Odysseus is his ideal."

In 1921 Capablanca, who got honorary pay from the Cuban government won the world championship against Lasker, who was ill-prepared and suffered from the heat in Havana. He won by 4:0 with 10 draws. In 1927 he lost against Alekhine by 3:6 with 25 draws. Beforehand just about everybody saw in Capablanca the favorite for this "Match of the Century" in Buenos Aires. His fame was based on legendary tournament successes – he took first place in 1911 in San Sebastián, in 1922 in London and in 1927 in New York, each time against the strongest international competition. Capablanca also came first as ex-world champion: Berlin 1928, Budapest 1929, Hastings 1930, Moscow 1936. Capablanca and his friends spent a lot of time trying to arrange a return game with Alekhine, who avoided a rematch and he knew why.

MAX (MACHGIELIS) EUWE, born in Amsterdam in 1901 and died 1981, was World Champion from 1935 to 1937. He was a mathematician and as a chess player also had a scientific streak. His systematic approach to the game is evident in his extensive work on openings and even more so in his book *Middle play,* because this phase of the game is much more difficult to divide into categories than the opening or the end game. Euwe was no pedant, however, and he had high respect for the psychological aspects. That is why he had a preference for duels.

Nearly everyone thought Euwe would be defeated when he challenged Alekhine, who was then regarded as unbeatable, and even more so because Euwe had lost two matches against Bogolyubov and one against Capablanca. But Euwe won. Later he said that he took the field against the World Champion in a very relaxed training mood and that might have been the reason that he won 9:8 with 13 draws. But two years later, during the return match, he played tensely and lost by 4:10 with 11 draws. Euwe is among those who were hampered in the full exploitation of their prime years by the Second World War. Later he became Professor of Cybernetics and the President of the World Chess Federation, which he led between 1970 and 1978.

ROBERT "BOBBY" JAMES FISCHER was born in Brooklyn, New York, in 1943 and was more consumed by the will to win than virtually any other player. His ambition was combined with the strictest professionalism. Fischer regarded the game as a tough job, devoting himself to chess to the exclusion of all adolescent activities. He set a high standard of professionalism: to be perfect in the positional game as well in the combinative game and to shine in the theory of openings, as well as in the technique of the endgame. This attitude reminds one of Botvinnik, but Fischer was much more imaginative. He is the creator of many sparkling games. Fischer was notorious for his small repertoire of openings. Any opponent could work out in advance how Fischer would react to certain moves, but even though he seemed to throw himself into every trap, he very quickly gained control of the game because he had thought more deeply about the most commonplace variations than his opponents. At fifteen, this boy who came from a poor background became the youngest grand master in world history. He was a self-made, first with regard to an indifferent American public, and then in the presence of a phalanx of Soviet grand masters who wanted to prevent his rise to the top. Fischer never played on a Saturday for religious reasons, and held the "sch" of his German-Jewish forbears' name in great honor.

Fischer had some early tournament, victories but his real strength became apparent during the preliminary rounds for the World Championships in 1972. He smashed the elite of the world at the Interzonal Tournament in Palma de Mallorca. After this, he beat Taimanov as well as Larsen 6:0. This is how it happened that Fischer won 21 difficult matches in succession, which no grand master had equaled. After he had defeated Petrosyan in Buenos Aires in 1971, he beat the World Champion Boris Spassky by 7:3 and 11 draws in Reykjavik in 1972. Having reached the pinnacle of the chess world, he withdrew and refused to defend the title against Karpov in 1975. Fat cheques and first class tournament conditions were part of his concept of chess professionalism.

Fischer made many demands for which he was ridiculed, chided and accused of being an eccentric. However, many of those demands are taken for granted today.

ANATOLY KARPOV, was born in Leningrad in 1951 and became World Champion by a red-tape decision in 1975 when Robert Fischer refused to defend his title. Karpov who had won three candidates' competitions, was awarded the title by FIDE. The Russian was sensitive about winning the title by default and proved to be a hard-working World Champion. He traveled from tournament to tournament and usually managed to win first place. As an indication of his many successes, here are the results that he gained at the annual Interpolis Tournament in Tilburg. Within 12 years Karpov participated 7 times, in the years 1977, 1979, 1980, 1982, 1983 and 1988, he placed first in spite of extremely strong competition and only once, in 1986, did he come third. Regarding his matches, Karpov, who as a candidate in 1974 beat Polugayevsky and Spassky in superior style, nearly lost to Viktor Korchnoi, who was twenty years older. This man challenged him in 1978 and 1981. Karpov won the first of these two World Championship matches in Baguio City by the skin of his teeth, 6:5 with 10 draws. In 1984–85 Karpov, the Youth World Champion of 1969, had to test his strength against the Youth World Champion of 1980, Garry Kasparov. The one who won six games first would be the winner. The battle that lasted for months, was broken off after 48 games by the FIDE President, Campomanes, with the agreement of Karpov, who was leading 5:3. Six months later, after Karpov had fully recovered the second match was held in Moscow, and Karpov lost his title by 3:5 with 16 draws.

Karpov is a versatile man, experienced in nearly all areas of psychology and political tactics as well, but he is not a risk taker. He waits with great patience for his adversary to make a mistake, even if it is a very small one, and then he makes the most of it by all the rules at his disposal. Besides this he is a lover of harmonious positions, which he attempts to develop deliberately. A clear move is the ideal of this great player.

GARRY KASPAROV was born in Baku in 1963 and has been the World Champion since 1985. He saw himself as the opposite of Karpov from the beginning. At the board Kasparov believed a player should be not just perfect but also inventive, not just careful but also take the incentive, not just cautious, but also daring. Kasparov wanted to tip Karpov off the World Champion's throne as soon as possible, and he actually achieved this rocketlike rise. In the tournaments of Bugojno in 1982 and Nikšić in 1983, which were studded with first-class players, he placed first, presenting himself to the chess world as the new, man to beat. In the Candidates competitions of the years 1983 and

1984 he beat Belyavsky, Korchnoi and Smyslov one after the other with convincing style. The World Championship match against Karpov went on for a long time and was broken off at the point where Kasparov, who had fallen behind, had recovered lost ground. The challenger denounced this FIDE decision as a nasty maneuver on the part of Karpov and his sympathiser, the FIDE President, Florencio Campomanes.

In the second Moscow contest, in 1985, Kasparov won by 5:3 with 16 draws, gained the title and became the youngest World Champion in chess history. Due to an absurd ruling, the two contestants had to play two further World Championship Games against each other in 1986 and 1987. The first theatres were London and Leningrad — Kasparov won by 5:4 with 15 draws. In the second match in Seville he only managed a dead heat, 4:4 with 16 draws, which according to an old custom is judged as the defeat of the challenger. Kasparov's game is fascinating. It is based on the ability to calculate many variations in the shortest possible time. His calculations are not without inaccuracies, but these cannot be capitalized by his opponents in the short time available for reflection. With regard to his style, Kasparov's favorite word is "fantasy."

PAUL KERES, who was born in 1916 in Navra (Estonia), and died in 1975 on a flight home from Canada, is the biggest loser in chess history. He began as a correspondence chess player and bold combinative player and had such tournament successes before the Second World War that a World Championship Match against Alekhine was in the cards, but it never came to that. After the war, Keres perfected his positional play, so that he had the ideal style and was able to keep his unusually strong command of the game over decades. The elegant grand master fought repeatedly for the right to challenge the World Champion and lost by a hair four times over. First prizes: Semmering 1937, AVRO Tournament, the Netherlands 1938 (shared with Reuben Fine), Margate 1939, Budapest 1952, Hastings 1965, and Bamberg 1968.

EMANUEL LASKER, who was born in 1868 in Berlinchen near Berlin and died in New York in 1941, was World Champion for 27 years from 1894 to 1921, which was a record. He was a first-rate tactician. He took over the principles of strategy from Steinitz, whom he beat in New York, Philadelphia and Montreal by 10:5 with 4 draws. Lasker's secret was practical psychology. For him chess was a battle, not between White and Black but between two heads, two souls, two hearts. Lasker sought to explore and make use of his opponent's weaknesses. Often he would choose the second or third strongest move, because this was the most unpleasant one for that particular opponent.

Lasker strove, not for beauty, but for expediency. In 1910 he would have lost the title in a sensational game had he not managed to trick his opponent, the phlegmatic Carl Schlechter, into making a risky attack. For it was Lasker's style to force his opponent to use a style that did not suit him. His contemporaries did not see through this and held Lasker's successes to be a kind of magic. He won countless games from what were, objectively speaking, hopeless positions, because he could wait till his opponent made mistakes either because of high-spiritedness or impatience. Lasker defended his title against Frank Marshall and Carl Schlechter, twice also David Janowski and twice also Siegbert Tarrasch. In 1921 he gave up the crown to Capablanca. Lasker's greatest tournament successes were St. Petersburg 1895–96, Nuremberg 1896, London 1899, Paris 1900, St. Petersburg 1914 and New York 1924. Even as a sixty-seven-year-old, he made third place in a strong Moscow international tournament in 1935. Lasker was a passionate mathematician and doctor of philosophy. He emigrated from Germany at the start of the Hitler period.

FRANK MARSHALL, who was born in 1877 in New York and died there in 1944, was the greatest chess player of all time, if one goes on bright ideas, mentally rich combinations and a never tiring swing. He was a combinative player who sought an open position so that he could attack his opponent. He never tired of rough tournament play. Marshall might well have asked himself the question that an old fighter must consider, namely, is a draw more valuable than a defeat. People like Marshall must continue to be around if chess is to remain popular. He won first prize in Cambridge Springs in 1904, in Nuremberg in 1906, in Düsseldorf in 1908 and in Havana in 1913. He founded the Marshall Chess Club in a brownstone in Greenwich Village, New York City.

PAUL MORPHY, who was born in 1837 in New Orleans and died there in 1884, appears to posterity to be the personification of eternal youth. His style, secretive moodiness and, most especially, the comet-like course of his career were romantic. His triumphal march consisted of only one European trip from June 1858 to April 1859. Before this tournament Morphy had passed one exam as a lawyer and impressed the local giants of New York. After this he wanted to hear less and less of the game that had also made him famous in his homeland. He doubted himself and the purpose of life. Even though his pleasant outward appearance and winning ways marked him as a potential celebrity, he withdrew more and more.

He proved himself to be the greatest player of the 19th century. In contests he beat Janos Jakob Löwenthal, David Harrwitz and Augustus Mongredien. The famous Howard Staunton avoided comparison of his strength to Morphy's, but Adolf Anderssen, Morphy's equal, presented himself for competition. Morphy beat him in Paris by 7:2 with 2 draws.

Amateurs have always been charmed by Morphy's games. But only years later did the professionals realised that strategic conceptions, which were only to be formulated much later, lay behind the lovely combinations which Morphy even then, had intuitively seen and played. The Hungarian grand master, Géza Maróczy, a truly quiet positional player of a totally different temperament from Morphy, called him "The Chosen of the Chosen."

AARON NIMZOWITSCH, who was born in 1886 in Riga and died in 1935 in Copenhagen, is, besides Tarrasch, the most highly regarded theoretician of our century. Nimzowitsch, in an acid and amusing style, turned the present conception of the game upside down in many essays and in the book, *My System.* He eulogized the pressed position, advised against attack, and refused to occupy the center with pawns because one can control it better by using pieces at a distance. When the chess world discovered the conservative elements in such revolutionary theories and, furthermore, forgave the author some of his exaggerations, Nimzowitsch became a modern classic. What he wrote about the handling of pawn chains, about the method of covering particular pieces a number of times, about the art of the blockade and about the technique of restraint has become general knowledge today.

Nimzowitsch was an important openings theoretician. Many variations carry his name. The Nimzowitsch Opening (1.e4 Ktc6) still appears ludicrous, but the Nimzowitsch Defence (1.d4 Ktf6 2.c4 e6 3.Ktc3 Bb4) is one of the most important openings of all. Nimzowitsch was also a great practitioner, even if his best games are very complicated and difficult to understand. His tactical ability was also praised by Alekhine. The tournament results were not always in keeping with his immense ability. His greatest success was getting the first place ahead of Capablanca, Spielmann and Rubinstein in Karlsbad in 1929.

TIGRAN PETROSYAN, who was born in Tbilisi in 1929 and was World Champion from 1963 to 1969, was the title holder who raised the least enthusiasm. He did not enter the picture as the creator of great thoughts about chess, but as a consistent obstacle to them. Naturally nobody becomes and remains a world champion by doing nothing. Petrosyan was a born opponent, who with tough patience and enviable caution procured the best squares for his men and slowly but surely out-maneuvered his attacker. "One must beware of unnecessary excitement," was his slogan. In the tournaments luck smiled and frowned at the Armenian. Often he did not lose even one game, but he still did not make it to the top of the table. In championship duels he beat Botvinnik in 1963 by 5:2 with 15 draws and Spassky in 1966 by 4:3 with 17 draws. He lost the next world championship contest against Spassky on his 40th birthday.

RICHARD RÉTI (1889–1929) the Czechoslovakian grand master was seen as one of the greatest representatives of the game in his time. The so-called "Hypermodern Chess School," a phrase invented by Tartakover, was the mark of a new direction in style, which differed from Tarrasch's mode of play, with the attack on the pawn center of the opponent by fianchetto bishops. Réti became a professional player after completing his studies in mathematics. Only in 1920, which was relatively late, did the international chess world first become aware of him. (He won first place in Amsterdam ahead of Maróczy and Tartakover and two places in Göteborg ahead of Rubinstein and Bogolyubov.) In 1924, he dealt Capablanca his first defeat, and in 1925 he beat Alekhine's world record in simultaneous blindfold play, taking on 29 opponents and winning 21 games with only two defeats. Réti bolstered the modern game in the books *Master of the Chess Board* (1930) and *New Ideas in Chess* (1922). This grand master, who died relatively young, was one of the most brilliant chess players in the first half of this century.

AKIBA RUBINSTEIN, who was born in 1882 in Stawiski in Poland and died in Antwerp in 1961, was the greatest artist of the endgame. Originally Rubinstein was to have become a rabbi. He was a quiet, unobtrusive man, who, in his best years played a virtually impeccable but somewhat monotonous game. In the last three decades of his life, he did not appear in public anymore, but before the First World War even the strongest feared him. He won first prize in Karlsbad in 1907, in San Sebastián in 1912, in Pistyan in 1912 and in Vienna in 1922.

VASSILY SMYSLOV, who was born in Moscow in 1921, was World Champion from 1957–1958 and perfected a style that was difficult to label. Euwe wrote that "it is not easy to say where his particular strength lies." From this one can gather that Smyslov was not excessive in any area. He loved the positional game, but he was a strong, robust, goal-oriented player. If the right moment came, he could strike like the greatest tactician. Smyslov fought Botvinnik for the World Championship three times: in 1954 he failed, because he only managed a dead heat, in 1957 he won the title, which he lost again in a return game in 1958. Smyslov would also have liked to have used his baritone voice to become a opera singer. Some authors say that he was melancholy. Smyslov won many tournaments but only two exceptional ones: the Candidate Tournaments in Zurich (1953) and in Amsterdam (1956). Being the distinguished end-game player that he was, he wrote the book *Theory of Rook End Games* with Löwenfisch.

BORIS SPASSKY, who was born in Leningrad in 1937, was World Champion from 1969 to 1972. He is a natural, not very hard working player, but of robust physical and psychological constitution, a practical man and a pragmatist, lacking in subtlety, but resourceful and tough. No demon hurries him, and depression has never clouded his life. Spassky was lucky. When he was at the peak of his ability, no genius got in his way. Forty years earlier another sturdy player, Efim Bogolyubov, failed against Alekhine, so now in 1969, Spassky overcame the title defender, Petrosyan, by 6:4 with 13 draws. Three years earlier he would not have beaten the same opponent, but at that time he won one of the bestmanned tournaments in history. After 1970 Spassky's playing strength dwindled visibly. When he came off second best against Bobby Fischer in 1972, there was not a great deal of surprise, generally.

WILHELM STEINITZ, who was born in 1836 in Prag and died in New York in 1900, was World Champion from 1866 to 1894. As the founder of the positional game, he is the father of modern chess. Steinitz taught that attacks are useless as long as the constellation is in balance. When this is lost, the attack must follow immediately, as the favorable situation will probably not recur. This cannot be an unspecific attack; on the contrary, the lever must be applied at exactly the weakest point. The somewhat dry Steinitz, who grasped these basic laws from a rational, rather than an intuitive base as Morphy did, was more than a match for his most temperamental and brilliant contemporaries.

In 1866 in London, Steinitz declared himself World Master, after he had beaten Anderssen by 8:6 without a single draw. In the first official World Championship Match in 1886 in New York and St. Louis, Steinitz defeated the Pole, Johannes Hermann Zukertort, by 10:5 with 5 draws. Steinitz defended his title against Isidor Gunsberg and twice against Michail Chigorin till he lost to Lasker in 1894. Steinitz won first prizes in the tournaments in London in 1872, in Vienna in 1873 and in Vienna again in 1882. Steinitz lived off the prizes he won, but not very well. When he did not win a prize in London in 1899 for the first time since his youth, he was economically ruined and psychologically broken. His life ended in a mental asylum.

MIKAIL TAL, who was born in 1936 in Riga, was World Champion from 1960 to 1961. He was called the "King of the Combination," also the "Magician" and the "Wizard." He developed a style that the professional world of chess thought was typical of the 19th century and no longer applicable in modern, overly careful, incessantly defensive grand master chess. Tal's ideas rushed through the chess world like a whirlwind. They were unorthodox, cheeky, extremely risky and crowned with success again and again. Tal's trademark was the unexpected, almost suicidal sacrifice of a piece, which tore open the constellation of the opponent but presented both parties with abundant problems. But even his mistaken sacrifices fulfilled a practical purpose because refutation could be achieved only after lengthy analysis, which could not, in many circumstances, be carried out over the board. One or two irritated grand masters therefore spoke of "bluff" or "hocus-pocus." Tal, who left the elite of the world in the dust in the great tournaments of Portoróz (1958) and Zurich (1959), could take such remarks with a shrug. But when he beat the World Champion Botvinnik by 6:2 with 13 draws, it was clear that great combinations are exceptional and that even "the magician" cannot make a rule out of an exception. Tal was, at the time, the youngest World Champion in history, but he lost the return match by 5:10 with 6 draws and since then has seldom reached his former legendary stature.

SIEGBERT TARRASCH, who was born in 1862 in Breslau and died in 1934 in Nuremberg, was the greatest chess teacher. He, like no other, made chess popular because he could make the most difficult train of thought accessible to his students. Tarrasch was a medical doctor, an educated man and a humanist, who wrote exquisite and sometimes sarcastic German. From Tarrasch, one can learn how to develop pieces, to open lines, to make outposts and to take aim at "targets." His tip to leave the rooks behind and not in front of one's own and the opponent's pawns became famous. Tarrasch believed that every correct move was also beautiful and insisted that in every particular position there is a move that is better than all the others. The idea of choosing the move according to one's opponent did not occur to him, which is why he never really understood Lasker to whom he lost the title match by 3:8 with 5 draws in 1908 in Düsseldorf. Certain misjudgements, such as the underestimation of the pressed position or the rejection of certain openings have been unfairly chalked up to Tarrasch. The *Praeceptor Germaniae* was not such a terrible dogmatist as some claim. Innumerable students have learned from his books, *The Chess Game* or *Three Hundred Chess Games*. His influence also rested upon his undeniable practical success. Considering that international tournaments were infrequent in his day, he won a remarkable number: Breslau in 1889, Manchester in 1890, Dresden in 1892, Leipzig in 1894, Vienna in 1898, Monte Carlo in 1903 and Ostende in 1907.

THE WORLD CHAMPIONSHIPS

A World Champion is determined in the Chess tournaments organized by FIDE. Since Wilhelm Steinitz defeated Johann Hermann Zukertort in the first officially acknowledged World championship in 1886, the tournament organization has gone through many changes. Up until 1946, the current World Master chose his own opponent when defending his title. Since the death of Alexander Alekhine in 1946, FIDE has been the decision-making body. Since 1948, qualification tournaments have been held every three years.

MEN

1886 – 1894: Wilhelm Steinitz
1886 in New York, St. Louis and New Orleans: Steinitz – Zukertort 12½:7½ (+10, –5, = 5).
1889 in Havana: Steinitz – Chigorin 10½: 6½ (+10, –6, = 1).
1890/91 in New York: Steinitz – Gunsberg 10½:8½ (+6, –4, = 9).
1892 in Havana: Steinitz – Chigorin 12½: 10½ (+10, –8, = 5).

1894 – 1921 Emanuel Lasker
1894 in New York, Philadelphia and Montreal: Steinitz – Lasker 7:12 (+5, –10, = 4).
1896/97 in Moscow: Lasker – Steinitz 12½: 4½ (+10, –2, = 5).
1907 in New York, Philadelphia, Memphis, Chicago and Baltimore: Lasker – Marshall 11½:3½ (+8, –0, =).

1908 in Düsseldorf and Munich: Lasker – Tarrasch 10½:5½ (+8, –3, = 5).
1909 in Paris: Lasker – Janowski 8:12 (+7, –1, = 2).
1919 in Vienna and Berlin: Lasker – Schlechter 5:5 (+1, –1, = 8).
1910 in Berlin: Lasker – Janowski 9½:1½ (+8, –0, = 3).

1921 – 1927: José Raúl Capablanca
1921 in Havana: Lasker – Capablanca 5:9 (+0, –4, = 10).

1927 – 1948: Alexander Alekhine and Machgielis Euwe
1927 in Buenos Aires: Capablanca – Alekhine 15½:18½ (+3, –6, = 25).
1929 in Germany and Holland: Alekhine – Bogolyubov 15½:9½ (+11, –5, = 9).

1934 in Germany: Alekhine – Bogolyubov 15½:10½ (+8, −3, = 15).
1935 in Holland: Alekhine – Euwe 14½:15½ (+8, −9, = 13).
1937 in Holland: Euwe – Alekhine 9½:15½ (+4, −10, = 11).

1948 – 1963: Michail Botvinnik, Vassily Smyslov, Mikail Tal
1948 in The Hague and Moscow (5 competitors, each against each, 5 games): 1. Botvinnik 14 p.; 2. Smyslov 11 p.; 3.–4. Keres, Reshevsky 10½ p.; 5. Euwe 4 p.
1951 in Moscow: Botvinnik – Bronstein 12:12 (+5, −5, = 14).
1954 in Moscow: Botvinnik – Smyslov 12:12 (+7, −7, = 10).
1957 in Moscow: Botvinnik – Smyslov 9½:12½ (+3, −6, = 13).
1958 in Moscow: Smyslov – Botvinnik 10½:12½ (+5, −7, = 11).
1960 in Moscow: Botvinnik – Tal 8½:12½ (+2, −6, = 13).
1961 in Moscow: Tal – Botvinnik 8:13 (+5, −10, = 6).

1963 – 1972: Tigran Petrosyan and Boris Spassky
1963 in Moscow: Botvinnik – Petrosyan 9½:12½ (+2, −5, = 15).
1966 in Moscow: Petrosyan – Spassky 12½:11½ (+4, −3, = 17).
1969 in Moscow: Petrosyan – Spassky 10½:12½ (+4, −6, = 13).

1972 – 1975: Robert James Fischer
1972 in Reykjavik: Spassky – Fischer 8½:12½ (+3, −7, = 11).

1975 – 1984: Anatoli Karpov
1975 in Manila: Fischer – Karpov (Fischer refused to defend his title against Karpov).
1978 in Baguio: Karpov – Korchnoi 6:5 (+6, −5, = 21).
1981 in Meran: Karpov – Korchnoi 6:2 (+6, −2, = 10).

From 1984: Garry Kasparov
1984 in Moscow: Karpov – Kasparov 5:3 (+5, −3, = 40).
1985 in Moscow: Karpov – Kasparov 11:13 (+3, −5, = 16).
1986 in London/Leningrad: Kasparov – Karpov: Return match 12½:11½ (+5, −4, = 15).
1987 in Sevilla: Kasparov – Karpov 12:12 (+4, −4, = 16).

WOMEN

1927 – 1944: Vera Menchik
1927 in London (during the Chess Olympics), 1930 in Hamburg, 1931 in Prague, 1933 in Folkestone, 1935 in Warsaw, 1937 in Stockholm, 1939 in Buenos Aires.

1949/50: Ludmila Rudenko
in Moscow

1953: Elizabeta Bykova
1953 in Leningrad: Rudenko – Bykova (+7, −5, = 22)

1956: Olga Rubtsova
1956 in Moscow: Triathlon: Elisabeta Bykova, Ludmilla Rudenko and Olga Rubtsova: 1. Rubtsova 10 p.; 2. Bykova 9½ p.; 3. Rudenko 4½ p.

1956 – 1959: Elizabeta Bykova
1958 in Moscow: Rubtsova – Bykova 5½:8½ (+7, −4, = 3)
1959 in Moscow: Bykova – Zworikina 8½:4½ (+6, −2, = 5)

1962 – 1975: Nona Gaprindaschwili
1962 in Moscow: Bykova – Gaprindaschwili 2:9 (+7, −0, = 4)
1965 in Riga: Gaprindaschwili – Kuschnir 8½:4½ (+7, −3, = 3)
1969 in Tiblisi/Moscow: Gaprindaschwili – Kuschnir 8½:4½ (+6, −2, = 5)
1972 in Riga: Gaprindaschwili – Kuschnir 8½:7½ (+5, −4, = 7)
1975 in Picunda/Tiblisi: Gaprindaschwili – Alexandria 8½:3½ (+8, −3, = 1)

1978 – 1988: Maya Chiburdanidze
1978 in Picunda: Gaprindaschwili – Chiburdanidze 6½:8½ (+4, −9, = 9)
1981 in Borzomi/Tiblisi: Chiburdanidze – Alexandria 8:8 (+4, −4, = 8)
1984 in Wolgograd: Chiburdanidze – Lewitina 8:5 (+5, −2, = 7)
1986 in Sofia/Borzomi: Chiburdanidze – Achmilovskaja 8½:5½
1988 in Talavi/Georgia (USSR): Chiburdanidze – Joseliani 8½:7½

THE CHESS OLYMPICS

In 1924 the first Team World Championship was held in Paris. The first official Chess Olympics were not organized by FIDE until 1927. The only break in the Olympics occurred in the years during and immediately following the Second World War, i.e. 1939 to 1950. From 1957 there have also been Chess Olympics for women.

MEN

1927 London (16 nations)
1. Hungary 40 p. (Marózy, Nagy, Vajda, Steiner A., Havasi); 2. Denmark 38,5 p.; 3. Great Britain 36,5 p.

1928 The Hague (17 nations)
1. Hungary 44 p. (Nagy, Steiner A., Vajda, Havasi); 2. USA 39,5 p.; 3. Poland 37 p.

1930 Hamburg (18 nations)
1. Poland 48,5 p. (Rubinstein, Tartakover, Przepiorka, Makarczyk, P. Frydman); 2. Hungary 47 p.; 3. Germany 44,5 p.

1931 Prague (19 nations)
1. USA 48 p. (Kashdan, Marshall, Dake, Horowitz, H. Steiner); 2. Poland 47 p.; 3. Czechoslovakia 46,5 p.

1933 Folkestone, USA (15 nations)
1. USA 39 p. (Kashdan, Marshall, Fine, Dake, Simonson); 2. Czechoslovakia 37,5 p.; 3. Sweden 34 p.

1935 Warsaw (20 nations)
1. USA 54 p. (Fine, Marshall, Kupchik, Dake, Horowitz); 2. Sweden 52,5 p.; 3. Poland 52 p.

1937 Stockholm (19 nations)
1. USA 54,5 p. (Reshevsky, Fine, Kashdan, Marshall, Horowitz); 2. Hungary 48,5 p.; 3. Poland 47 p.

1939 Buenos Aires (26 nations)
1. Great Germany 36 p. (Eliskases, P. Michel, Engels, Becker, Reinhardt); 2. Poland 35,5 p.; 3. Estonia 33,5 p.

1950 Dubrovnik (16 nations)
1. Yugoslavia 45,5 p. (Gligorić, Pirč, Trifunović, Rabar, Vidmar jun., Puc); 2. Argentina 43,5 p.; 3. GRF 40,5 p.

1952 Helsinki (25 nations)
1. Soviet Union 21 p. (Keres, Smyslov, Bronstein, Geller, Boleslavsky, Kotov); 2. Argentina 19,5 p.; 3. Yugoslavia 19 p.

1954 Amsterdam (26 nations)
1. Soviet Union 34 p. (Botvinnik, Smyslov, Bronstein, Keres, Geller, Kotov); 2. Argentina 27 p.; 3. Yugoslavia 26,5 p.

1956 Moscow (34 nations)
1. Soviet Union 31 p. (Botvinnik, Smyslov, Keres, Bronstein, Taimanov, Geller); 2. Yugoslavia 26,5 p.; 3. Hungary 26,5 p.

1958 Munich (36 nations)
1. Soviet Union 34,5 p. (Botvinnik, Smyslov, Keres, Bronstein, Tal, Petrosyan); 2. Yugoslavia 26 p.; 3. Argentina 25,5 p.

1960 Leipzig (40 nations)
1. Soviet Union 34 p. (Tal, Botvinnik, Keres, Korchnoi, Smyslov, Petrosyan); 2. USA 29 p.; 3. Yugoslavia 27 p.

1962 Varna, Bulgaria (37 nations)
1. Soviet Union 31,5 p. (Botvinnik, Petrosyan, Spassky, Keres, Geller, Tal); 2. Yugoslavia 28 p.; 3. Argentina 26 p.

1964 Tel Aviv (50 nations)
1. Soviet Union 36,5 p. (Petrosyan, Botvinnik, Smyslov, Keres, Stein, Spassky); 2. Yugoslavia 32 p.; 3. GFR 30,5 p.

1966 Havanna (52 nations)
1. Soviet Union 39,5 p. (Petrosyan, Spassky, Tal, Stein, Korchnoi, Polugayevsky); 2. USA 34,5 p.; 3. Hungary 33,5 p.

1968 Lugano, Switzerland (53 nations)
1. Soviet Union 39,5 p. (Petrosyan, Spassky, Korchnoi, Geller, Polugayevsky, Smyslov); 2. Yugoslavia 31 p.; 3. Bulgaria 30 p.

1970 Siegen, GFR (60 nations)
1. Soviet Union 27,5 p. (Spassky, Petrosyan, Korchnoi, Polugayevsky, Smyslov, Geller); 2. Hungary 26,5 p.; 3. Yugoslavia 26 p.

1972 Skopje, Yugoslavia (63 nations)
1. Soviet Union 42 p. (Petrosyan, Korchnoi, Smyslov, Tal, Karpov); 2. Hungary 40,5 p.; 3. Yugoslavia 38 p.

1974 Nice (73 nations)
1. Soviet Union 46 p. (Spassky, Petrosyan, Tal, Karpov, Korchnoi, Kusmin); 2. Yugoslavia 37,5 p.; 3. USA 36,5 p.

1976 Haifa (48 nations)
1. USA 37 p. (Byrne R., Evans, Kavalek, Tarjan, Lombardy, Commons); 2. The Netherlands 36,5 p.; 3. Great Britain 35,5 p. (boycotted by the states of the Eastern bloc)

1978 Buenos Aires (66 nations)
1. Hungary 37 p. (Portisch, Ribli, Sax, Adorjan, Csom, Vadasz); 2. Soviet Union 36 p.; 3. USA 35 p.

1980 Malta (82 nations)
1. Soviet Union 39 p. (Karpov, Tal, Polugayevsky, Geller, Balaschov, Kasparov); 2. Hungary 39 p.; 3. Yugoslavia 35 p.

1982 Lucerne (92 nations)
1. Soviet Union 42,5 p. (Karpov, Kasparov, Polugayevsky, Belyavsky, Tal, Yusupov); 2. Czechoslovakia 36 p.; 3. USA 35,5 p.

1984 Thessalonica (88 nations)
1. Soviet Union 41 p. (Belyavsky, Polugayevsky, Waganian, Tukmakov, Yusupov, Sokolov); 2. Great Britain 37 p.; 3. USA 35 p.

1986 Dubai (108 nations)
1. Soviet Union 40 p. (Kasparov, Karpov, Sokolov, Yusupov, Waganian, Tscheschkovskij); 2. Great Britain 39,5 p.; 3. USA 38,5 p.

1988 Thessalonica (107 nations)
1. Soviet Union 40,5 p. (Kasparov, Karpov, Yusupov, Belyavsky, Ehlvest, Ivancuk); 2. Great Britain 34,5 p.; 3. The Netherlands 34,5 p.

WOMEN

1957 Emmen, Switzerland (21 nations)
1. Soviet Union 10,5 p.; 2. Rumania 10,5 p.; 3. GDR 10 p.

1963 Split, Yugoslavia (15 nations)
1. Soviet Union 25 p.; 2. Yugoslavia 24,5 p.; 3. GDR 21 p.

1966 Oberhausen, GFR (14 nations)
1. Soviet Union 22 p.; 2. Rumania 20,5 p.; 3. GDR 17 p.

1969 Lublin, Poland (15 nations)
1. Soviet Union 26 p.; 2. Hungary 20,5 p.; 3. Czechoslovakia 19 p.

1972 Skopje, Yugoslavia (23 nations)
1. Soviet Union 11,5 p.; 2. Rumania 8 p., 3. Hungary 8 p.

1974 Medellin, Colombia (26 nations)
1. Rumania 13,5 p.; 2. Soviet Union 13,5 p.; 3. Bulgaria 13 p.

1976 Haifa (23 nations)
1. Israel 17 p.; 2. Great Britain 11,5 p.; 3. Spain 11,5 p.

Buenos Aires (32 nations)
1. Soviet Union 16 p.; 2. Hungary 11 p.; 3. GFR 11 p.

1980 Malta (42 nations)
1. Soviet Union 32,5 p.; 2. Hungary 32 p.; 3. Poland 26,5 p.

1982 Lucerne (45 nations)
1. Soviet Union 33 p.; 2. Rumania 30 p.; 3. Hungary 36 p.

1984 Thessalonica (51 nations)
1. Soviet Union 32 p.; 2. Bulgaria 27,5 p.; 3. Rumania 27 p.

1986 Dubai (49 nations)
1. Soviet Union 33,5 p.; 2. Hungary 29 p.; 3. Rumania 28 p.

1988 Thessalonica (56 nations)
1. Hungary 33 p.; 2. Soviet Union 32,5 p.; 3. Yugoslavia 28 p.

BIBLIOGRAPHY

Botvinnik, M.: One Hundred Selected Games. New York 1982

Brace, R.: An Illustrated Dictionary of Chess. London 1977

Capablanca, J. R.: My Chess Career. New York

Chess: East and West, Past and Present. A Selection from the Gustavus A. Pfeiffer Collection. New York 1968

Chicco, A. and Porreca, G.: Il libro completo degli scacchi. Milan 1973

Eales, R.: Chess. The History of the Game. London 1985

Euwe, M.: From Steinitz to Fischer. Belgrade 1976

Faber, M.: Das Schachspiel in der europäischen Malerei und Graphik. Wiesbaden 1988

Fine, R.: The Psychology of the Chess Player. New York 1967

Finkenzeller, R.: Vom Schachspiel. Frankfurt 1988

Fischer, B.: Bobby Fischer's Games of Chess. London 1959.
My 60 Memorable Games. London 1969

Fondern, M. and others: Lexikon für Schachfreunde. Luzern 1980

Gizycki, J.: A History of Chess. London 1972

Golombek, H.: The Encyclopedia of Chess. London 1977

Graham, F. L.: Chess Sets. London 1968

Hooper, D. and Whyld, K.: The Oxford Companion to Chess. Oxford 1984

Keats, V.: Chessmen for Collectors. London 1985

Kotov, A. and Judovich, M.: The Soviet Chess School. Moscow 1983

Kruijswijk, K. W.: Chess – Bibliography and History (vol. 1). The Hague 1974

Linder, J. M.: U istokov sachmattnoj kultury. Moscow 1967

Lionnais, F. and Maget, E.: Dictionnaire des Échecs. Paris 1974

Mackett-Beeson, A. E. J.: Chessmen. London 1967

Pandolfini, B.: One-move Chess by the Champions. New York 1985
Bobby Fischer's outragious Chess Moves. New York 1985
Kasparov's Winning Chess Tactics. New York 1986

Petzold, J.: Das Königliche Spiel. Stuttgart 1987

Pfleger, H. and Metzing, H.: Schach. Hamburg 1984

Reinfeld, F.: The Development of a Chess Genius. New York

Réti, R.: Masters of the Chess-board. New York 1933

Steinitz, W.: The Modern Chess Instructor. Zürich 1984

Tal, M.: Tal – Botvinnik Match for the World Chess Championship 1960. London 1977

Taylor, M.: The Lewis Chessmen. London 1978

Unzicker, W.: Schach für Kenner. München 1985

Wade, R. G.: World Chess Championship. From Botvinnik to Kasparov. London 1986

Wichmann, H. and S.: Schach. Ursprung und Wandlung der Spielfigur in zwölf Jahrhunderten. München 1960

Wilson, F.: A Picture History of Chess. New York 1981

Winter, E. G.: World Chess Champions. Oxford 1981

PICTURE CREDIT

Herzog August Bibliothek, Wolfenbüttel: Endpaper, 26 left, 36 left, 108 left and right

Bayerisches Nationalmuseum, Munich: 91 left, 103 bottom, 114 top left, 115 bottom left

Bayerische Staatsbibliothek, Munich: 8, 42, 68, 106, 152, 173

BBC Hulton Picture Library, London: 124

By courtesy of Belser Faksimile Editions out of Biblioteca Apostolica Vaticana, Zurich: 26 right, 27, 157

Bibliothèque Nationale, Paris: 22, 49, 135 middle right

Collection Dr. Ernst and Sonya Böhlen, Switzerland: 9, 43, 63, 66, 70 bottom middle and right, 71 middle and right, 72 2nd and 3rd from left, 73 top left and middle, 73 bottom 3rd from left, 74 top left and right, 74 bottom 1st to 4th from left, 75 2nd and 3rd from left, 77 right, 78 (4 ×), 79 bottom 1st to 3rd and 6th from left, 80 2nd and 4th and 5th from left, 81 bottom 1st and 3rd and 5th from left, 82 top, 82 bottom 3rd and 4th from left, 83 top right, 83 bottom 2nd and 5th from left, 86 (4 ×), 87 top, 87 bottom 1st and 2nd from left, 88 bottom 2nd to 5th from left, 89 bottom, 90 bottom 3rd and 4th from left, 93 bottom 2nd – 4th from left, 94 top (2 ×), 94 bottom (2 ×), 98 bottom (4 ×), 99 top (2 ×), 99 bottom (3 ×), 100 top middle, 100 bottom left, 101 (3 ×), 103 top (4 ×), 104 (2 ×), 107, 109 bottom, 110 (3 ×), 111, 112 (3 ×), 113 (2 ×), 114 middle and bottom, 115 top and right, 116 (2 ×), 117 (2 ×), 120, 123, 127, 131, 167, 171

J. Braunschweiger, Lucerne: 180, 181

British Museum, London: Title page and 71 left, 90 bottom 1st from left, 93 bottom 1st from left, 100 right

Cabinet des Médailles, Paris: 69 left, 93 top (2 ×), 97

Hand prints of Clan-Presse, Schretstaken: 135 bottom right

Control Data, Frankfurt: 149 bottom

Domschatz Osnabrück: 70 bottom left, 84 top, 95 right

Dover Publications, Inc., Minneola: 32 right, 54 left

Archive EMB, Lucerne: 156 left

Biblioteca Escorial, Madrid: 15, 21, 23, 25, 109 top, 153 left, 154 bottom left, 170

Grovatta Ferruccio, Triest: 168

FIDE, Lucerne, 58 top right, 58 bottom right, 59

Forschungsbibliothek Gotha: 19, 177

Germanisches Nationalmuseum, Nürnberg: 70 top, 90 top, 93 bottom 5th from left, 102 bottom (2 ×)

Jerzy Gizycki, A History of Chess, The Abbey Library, London 1972: 29, 34 top, 35 middle and top, 36 right, 132/33 top, 133 bottom, 135 top right

Collection David Hafler, Philadelphia: 6 left, 7 right, 16 right, 17 left, 18 top, 69 right, 72 1st from left, 73 top right, 73 bottom 2nd and 4th from left, 75 1st and 4th from left, 82 bottom 1st and 2nd from left, 83 top left, 83 bottom 1st and 3rd and 4th from left, 87 bottom 4th from left, 92 (2 ×) and title page, 96 left, 98 top, 102 top, 165

Archive Hans-Joachim Hecht, Fürstenfeldbruck: 55 right

Hegner + Glaser Co., Munich: 149 top

Historisches Museum, Basle: 164 (M. Babey)

Horst von Irmer, International Picture Library, Munich: 105

Catherine Jaeg, Paris: 175 middle

Jiri Jiru, Brussels: 186, 187

Collection Karl Graf von Almeida, Starnberg: 81 bottom 4th from left and title page

Editions Dr. Horst Kerlikowsky, Munich: 44, 45

Kunstgewerbemuseum, Cologne: 81 bottom 2nd from left

Kunsthaus Zurich: 67

Kunstsammlungen zu Weimar: 76

Kyrkorna Church, S-Täby: 35 right

Archive LNN, Lucerne: 144 left, 146 bottom left, 147 bottom right

The Museum of London: 47, 95 left, 99 right

Musée du Louvre, Paris: 74 bottom 5th from left

Magnum, Paris: 169 (Barbey)

Editions les Maîtres, New York: 46/47

Manesse hand prints, facsimile of Public Library, Lucerne: 154 top, 155, 158/159

G. Marks foundation, Bremen: 60 bottom

Massmann, Geschichte des mittelalterlichen Deutschen Schachspiels, Leipzig 1836: 194 left top and bottom, 195 right, 196 left, 197 right, 198 left top and bottom, 199 right, 200 left

Metropolitan Museum of Art, New York: 172

Collection The Museum of Modern Art, New

York: 61 left

Motovun Tokyo: 182, 183

Archive Motovun Verlagsgesellschaft, Lucerne: 12, 64/65, 134 left (Othmar Baumli), 163 (Fox Talbot)

Beat Müller, CH-Fahrweid/Zurich: 52/53

Nationalmuseum Edinburgh: 82 bottom 5th from left, 89 top and title page

Nationalmuseum Kopenhagen: 77 left, 88 top, 91 right, 94 left

Museo Nazionale, Florence: 72 4th from left

Museo Nazionale, Naples: 73 bottom 1st from left

The New York Public Library, New York: 28

Editions Olms, Zurich: 10 left, 50 bottom 1st from left

Hannes Opitz, Lucerne: 14 left middle, 20 left and middle, 24 left and top, 37, 38/39, 126, 128, 129

Picture Library of Oesterreichische Nationalbibliothek, Vienna: 30 bottom left, middle and right, 31 top middle and right, 32 left, 50 top left, 50 bottom 2nd to 4th from left, 54 right, 56/57, 57 left and right, 58 left, 61 right, 139 left

Musée du Petit Palais, Paris: 151

Hans Pfannmüller: 46

Philadelphia Museum of Art: Louise and Walter Arensberg Collection: 134 top

Philidor: L'Analyse des Echecs: 30 top

John Phillips, New York: 118 bottom left

Picture Library Preussischer Kulturbesitz, Berlin: 34, 40/41, 162

Ringier Dokumentationszentrum, Zurich: 65 left, 185 (Lanz)

Rosenheimer Verlag: 166 (Fred Marcus)

Royal Asiatic Society, London: 13

Scala, Florence: 6/7 middle, 160, 161

Chess Agency Zurich (Rupp): 147 top right, 189, 192, 200/201

Die Schachwoche, CH-Sarmenstorf: 57 top, 143 right, 148 middle, 175 bottom, 188

Historical Museum, Stockholm: 84 bottom

Staatliche Museen, Berlin: 5, 11 right, 79 top, 85

Historical Museum, Moscow: 1 and 193

Städtische Galerie, Frankfurt: 90 bottom 2nd from left

Städtische Museen, Mannheim: 81 top

Stern Syndicat, Hamburg: 121 (Thomann), 139 right (Spill), 174, 191 (Moldvay)

Branislav Strugar, Belgrade: 118/119 (6 ×), 125, 136

Picture Library Süddeutscher Verlag, Munich: 51 top left, 51 bottom left and right, 51 top right, 55 top left, 55 bottom left and middle, 56 left, 57 middle, 60 top left, 130, 132 left, 134/135 middle, 138, 141 right, 142 left, 142 top middle and right, 143 left, 144 right, 145, 147 top left and middle, 148

TASS: 174 top left and right, 174 bottom, 175 top

Prehistoric Collection of University Tübingen: 96 right

Um-Dia-Verlag A. + M. Burges, Munich: 11 top middle

Vatican Museum: 11 bottom middle

Bonnie Waitzkin, New York: 184

Württ. Landesbibliothek, Stuttgart: 48

Xinhua, Beijing: 178, 179

INDEX OF NAMES